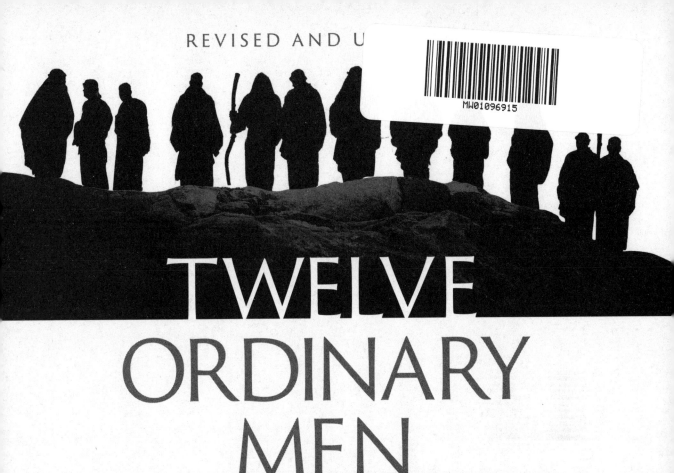

REVISED AND U...

MW01096915

TWELVE ORDINARY MEN

How JESUS Shaped HIS DISCIPLES for GREATNESS
and What HE WANTS to DO WITH YOU

WORKBOOK

BASED ON THE BOOK BY

JOHN MACARTHUR

HarperChristian Resources

Twelve Ordinary Men Workbook (Revised and Updated)
© 2025 by John MacArthur

Published in Grand Rapids, Michigan, by HarperChristian Resources. HarperChristian Resources is a regis-tered trademark of HarperCollins Christian Publishing, Inc.

Requests for information should be sent to customercare@harpercollins.com.

ISBN 978-0-310-17685-5 (softcover)
ISBN 978-0-310-17686-2 (ebook)

HarperChristian Resources titles may be purchased in bulk for church, business, fundraising, or ministry use. For information, please e-mail ResourceSpecialist@ChurchSource.com.

First Printing May 2025 / Printed in the United States of America

CONTENTS

A NOTE FROM
JOHN MacARTHUR

I have always been fascinated with the lives of the twelve apostles. Who isn't? The personality types of these men are familiar to us. They are just like us, and they are like other people we know. They are approachable. They are real and living characters we can identify with. Their faults and foibles, as well as their triumphs and endearing features, are chronicled in some of the most fascinating accounts of the Bible. These are men we *want* to know.

That's because they were perfectly ordinary men in every way. Not one of them was renowned for scholarship or great erudition. They had no track record as orators or theologians. In fact, they were outsiders as far as the religious establishment of Jesus' day was concerned. They were not outstanding because of any natural talents or intellectual abilities. On the contrary, they were all too prone to mistakes, misstatements, wrong attitudes, lapses of faith, and bitter failures—no one more so than the leader of the group, Peter. Even Jesus remarked that they were slow learners and somewhat spiritually dense (see Luke 24:25).

They spanned the political spectrum. One was a former Zealot—a radical, determined to overthrow Roman rule. But another had been a tax collector—virtually a traitor to the Jewish nation and in collusion with Rome. At least four, and possibly seven, were fishermen and close friends from Capernaum, probably having known one another from childhood. The others must have been tradesmen or craftsmen, but we are not told what they did before becoming followers of Christ. Most of them were from Galilee, an agricultural region at the intersection of trade routes. And Galilee remained their home base for most of Jesus' ministry—not (as some might think) Jerusalem in Judea, which was the political and religious capital of Israel.

Yet with all their faults and character flaws—as remarkably ordinary as they were—these men carried on a ministry after Jesus' ascension that left an indelible impact on the world. Their ministry continues to influence us today. God graciously empowered and used these men to inaugurate the spread of the gospel and to turn the world upside down (see Acts 17:6). Ordinary men—people like you and me—became the instruments by which Christ's message was carried to the ends of the earth. No wonder they are such fascinating characters.

These studies in the lives of the apostles have been a particular delight for me—and one of the most fruitful endeavors of my life. My greatest joy is preaching Christ. Eleven of these men shared that passion, devoted their lives to it, and triumphed in it against overwhelming opposition. They are fitting heroes and role models for us, despite their shortcomings. To study their lives is to get to know the men who were closest to Christ during His earthly life. To realize that they were ordinary people just like us is a great blessing. May the Spirit of Christ who taught them transform us the way He transformed them, into precious vessels fit for the Master's use. And may we learn from their example what it means to be disciples indeed.

— JOHN MACARTHUR

THE MEN JESUS CALLED:

OUTSTANDINGLY ORDINARY

No longer do I call you servants, for a servant does not know what his master is doing; but I have called you friends, for all things that I heard from My Father I have made known to you. You did not choose Me, but I chose you and appointed you that you should go and bear fruit, and that your fruit should remain.

JOHN 15:15–16

What comes to mind when you picture the twelve disciples? Perhaps the image is something similar to Leonardo da Vinci's famous painting *The Last Supper*, where the twelve men are dressed in fine clothing and look more like nobility than commoners. Or maybe the picture you see is of the larger-than-life saints with shining halos that are often depicted in European cathedrals. It's unfortunate the disciples have so often been put on marble pedestals or portrayed like this. It dehumanizes them. They were just twelve ordinary men, perfectly human in every way, and we shouldn't lose touch with who they really were.

Jesus, in fact, seems to have deliberately chosen men who were notable only for their ordinariness. This would have been unusual in his day. In the first century, a rabbi—a Jewish religious teacher—would have sought out only well-educated students to be his disciples. Jesus, however, did not choose His disciples based on their knowledge, or intrinsic abilities, or outstanding talents. Rather, He chose ordinary Galileans, who would have been deemed by Jewish society as low-class, rural, and uneducated. They were commoners.

The twelve disciples were, in many ways, just like us. They came from all different kinds of backgrounds like us. They were selected by Jesus from the unworthy and the unqualified—just like us. Their transformation into vessels of honor was solely the work of the Potter. These men "turned the world upside down" (Acts 17:6) because God worked in them to do it. So it is that we need to consider them not from their stained-glass or highly idealized images but as real living-and-breathing people. We need to get to know them as actual men and not as some kind of exalted figures from the pantheon of religious ritualism.

This not to undermine the importance of their office. The twelve disciples, in effect, became the true spiritual leaders of Israel. They were the ones to whom the Christian gospel was first entrusted. They became the foundation stones of the church, with "Jesus Christ Himself being the chief cornerstone" (Ephesians 2:20). However, those truths are heightened, not diminished, by the fact that these men were so ordinary.

STARTING OUT

Whether you know a little or a lot about the twelve disciples of Jesus, what do you hope will happen as you study the lives of these ordinary men in this study?

_____

_____

_____

_____

_____

_____

EXPLORING THE STORY

When you read the Gospels and Acts, it becomes evident that God's strategy for advancing His kingdom hinged on the twelve disciples. There was no backup plan if they failed. So, it is important to consider how these men were *called*, *trained*, and *tasked* for ministry. In this section, you will explore passages from the Bible that reveal how Jesus shaped these perfectly ordinary men into extraordinary representatives of God's kingdom.

The Calling of the Twelve

When Andrew encountered Jesus, he was already a disciple of John the Baptist (see John 1:35, 40).[1] However, when he heard his teacher say, "Behold the Lamb of God" (verse 36), he began to follow after Jesus. This was phase one of the calling of the Twelve—a call to *conversion*. It was a call to recognize Jesus as the true Lamb of God and embrace Him by faith.

Phase two was a call to *ministry*. Luke relates a story of how Jesus had just finished teaching the multitudes from Peter's boat near the shore of the Sea of Galilee. Jesus instructed Peter to launch out to the deep and put in his nets, and the resulting catch of fish overwhelmed the fishermen's nets (see 5:1–7). Jesus then said to Peter—and to James and John, who were with him—"From now on you will catch men" (verse 10). When the fishermen returned to the shore, "they forsook all and followed Him" (verse 11). From that point on, both sets of brothers—Peter and Andrew, and James and John—were inseparable from the Lord.

THE LAMB OF GOD

The use of a lamb for sacrifice was familiar to Jews. A lamb was used as a sacrifice during Passover (see Exodus 12:1–36); a lamb was led to the slaughter in the prophecies of Isaiah (see Isaiah 53:7); and a lamb was offered in the daily sacrifices of Israel (see Exodus 29:38–42; Numbers 28:1–8; see also Hebrews 10:5–7). John the Baptist used this expression as a reference to the ultimate sacrifice of Jesus on the cross to atone for the sins of the world, a theme which John the apostle carries throughout his writings (see John 19:36; Revelation 5:1–6; 7:17; 17:14) and that appears in other New Testament writings (see 1 Peter 1:19).[1]

Phase three was a call to *apostleship*. The word *apostle* comes from the Greek *apostolos*, which conveys the idea of an ambassador, delegate, or official representative. Jesus selected and appointed the Twelve to be apostles out of a larger group of disciples who followed Him (see Luke 6:12–16). The Twelve were different in that they were His delegates. They spoke with His authority, delivered His message, and exercised His authority.

Phase four was a call to *martyrdom*. After Jesus rose from the dead, He appeared to eleven of His disciples (for Judas had hanged himself after his betrayal) and told them, "Go therefore and make disciples of all the nations, baptizing them in the name of the Father and of the Son and of the Holy Spirit" (Matthew 28:19). This was, in effect, a call to martyrdom, as church history records that all of them except John were killed for their testimony.

- Read John 1:35–49. Phase one in the calling of the Twelve was *conversion*—recognizing Jesus as the Lord of all and embracing Him by faith. What are some of the examples of conversion found in this passage? What does Jesus' response to Nathanael indicate about His heart toward those who are more hesitant to accept Him at first as Lord?

  _____

  _____

  _____

  _____

  _____

- Read Luke 5:8–11. Phase two was a call to *ministry*. What do Simon Peter's response and the first words of Jesus in His call to the four fishermen reveal about being a disciple?

  _____

  _____

  _____

  _____

  _____

- Read Matthew 10:6–12. Phase three was a call to *apostleship*. How would the restrictions that Jesus specified help train these men for their future work?

  _____
  _____
  _____
  _____
  _____

- Read John 21:18–19. Phase four was a call to *martyrdom*. What did Jesus say in this passage about what the cost would be to Peter for being His disciple?

  _____
  _____
  _____
  _____
  _____

- Think about Jesus' call on your own life to be His disciple. Which of the following has been the most challenging for you—and why?

  1. Conversion (believing in Christ):

  2. Ministry (giving up your work to do the Lord's work):

3. Ambassadorship (representing Jesus in your world):

4. Discipleship and evangelism (living sacrificially and witnessing):

The Training of the Disciples

The twelve disciples had now abandoned their nets, forsaken their fields, and left the tax tables behind to follow after Jesus. The next eighteen months of their lives would be filled with training in ministry. In this, they had the example, wisdom, and instruction of Jesus perpetually before them as a guide. Still, the learning process proved to be difficult, for they could be amazingly thick-headed. They had to overcome many obstacles for their training to take place.

First, the disciples needed to gain *spiritual understanding*. We see this in the fact that Jesus often said things to them like, "Are you also still without understanding? Do you not yet understand?" (Matthew 15:16–17). Jesus addressed this lack of spiritual understanding by continuing to teach them. Even after His resurrection, He stayed with them for forty days "speaking of the things pertaining to the kingdom of God" (Acts 1:3).

Second, the disciples needed to obtain *greater faith*. At one point, Jesus said to them, "Why are you so fearful? How is it that you have no faith?" (Mark 4:40). This lack of faith on the disciples' part often left them unable to harness the power of God that was available to them. Jesus remedied this weakness by continuing to do miracles in their midst. The Gospels repeat that most of Jesus' miracles were not done primarily for the benefit of unbelievers but were done "in the presence of His disciples" so that their faith could be strengthened (John 20:30). Jesus later also sent the Holy Spirit to indwell and empower them (see Acts 1:8).

TRUE FAITH

Jesus said to His disciples, "I say to you, if you have faith as a mustard seed, you will say to this mountain, 'Move from here to there,' and it will move; and nothing will be impossible for you" (Matthew 17:20). True faith, by Christ's definition, always involves surrender to the will of God. Both the source and the object of all genuine faith—even the weak, mustard-seed variety—is God.[3]

Third, the disciples needed to learn *commitment*. The disciples were thrilled to follow after Jesus when the crowds were cheering and the miracles were being multiplied. But as soon as the first sign of real trouble came their way in the form of Jesus' arrest, they all forsook Him and fled (see Mark 14:50). Jesus responded to their proneness to defection by interceding for them in prayer. Shortly before His death, He prayed they would remain *ultimately* faithful to Him and that the Father would bring them to heaven (see John 17:11–26).

- Read Mark 4:10–12. What did Jesus do after teaching the crowds to provide His disciples with greater spiritual understanding?

  _____

  _____

  _____

  _____

- Read Matthew 17:14–21. Why did the disciples lack the power needed to cast the demon out of the boy? What did Jesus reveal about the power of faith?

  _____

  _____

  _____

  _____

- Read Mark 14:27–28. What did Jesus prophesy about His disciples' lack of commitment in following Him when the situation grew difficult for them?

  _____
  _____
  _____
  _____

- Read 1 Corinthians 2:1–5. What does Paul's humble admission in this passage tell you about what the mindset should be for a true disciple of Christ?

  _____
  _____
  _____
  _____

The Task of the Disciples

Jesus' training of the twelve disciples involved a kind of internship. He would send them out on short-term mission projects, and they would report back to Him on how things were going (see Luke 9:10; 10:17). Jesus graciously encouraged them, lovingly corrected them, patiently instructed them, and steadfastly invested His time and energy in them. The question is . . . *Why?* Why was it so important for these twelve men to be personally equipped by Christ?

Remember that God's strategy for advancing His kingdom hinged on the twelve disciples. They were common men, but they had been given uncommon tasks. These tasks included nothing less than providing the source of church doctrine, edifying the body of Christ, and serving as examples of virtue. Let's examine each of these in turn.

First, the disciples were tasked to be the *source of church doctrine*. Not only would they found the church and play a pivotal role in its leadership, but they would also be the channels through which most of the New Testament was given. They did not preach a human message but one that had been given to them by revelation from God. In fact, the written New Testament is nothing other than the Holy Spirit-inspired record of the apostles' teaching.

THE DISCIPLES' TRAINING PROGRAM

Notice the natural progression in the disciples' training program. At first, they simply follow Jesus, gleaning from His sermons and listening to His instructions along with a larger group of disciples. They apparently did not do this full-time but as opportunity allowed in the course of their regular lives. Next, Jesus calls them to leave everything and follow Him exclusively. Jesus then selects twelve men out of that group of full-time disciples, identifies them as apostles, and begins to focus most of His energies on their personal instruction. Later, He will gift them with authority and miracle power. Finally, He will send them out. At first, this involves them going out on short-term missions projects and reporting back. But when Jesus leaves to return to the Father, they will go out for good on their own.[4]

Second, the disciples were tasked with *edifying the church*. In Ephesians 4:11–12, the apostle Paul wrote, "[Jesus] Himself gave some to be apostles, some prophets, some evangelists, and some pastors and teachers, for the equipping of the saints for the work of ministry, for the edifying of the body of Christ." The twelve disciples were the original Christian teachers and preachers in the church. Their teaching, as recorded in the New Testament, is the only rule by which sound doctrine can be tested, even today.

Third, the disciples were tasked with being *examples of virtue*. In Ephesians 3:5, Paul calls them "holy apostles." They set a standard for godliness and spirituality and were the first examples for believers to emulate. They were men of character and integrity who set the standard for all who would subsequently become leaders in the church.

- Read 2 Timothy 4:2–4. What are Jesus' disciples everywhere tasked to do when it comes to preaching the gospel and equipping people with doctrine?

_____

_____

_____

_____

- Read Ephesians 4:29–32. What does Paul say in this passage about how followers of Jesus are to edify one another in the church?

  _____

  _____

  _____

  _____

- Read 1 Peter 1:13–16. How are disciples of Jesus tasked with being an example of virtue to the world? What does it mean to be "holy" in your conduct?

  _____

  _____

  _____

  _____

- What is the difference between a listener—someone who is simply part of the crowd—and a true disciple of Christ? What caused that shift in your life?

  _____

  _____

  _____

  _____

CONSIDERING YOUR STORY

Read 1 Corinthians 1:26–29. In Paul's day, the gospel was deemed by many to be a foolish message. The apostles were seen as unsophisticated preachers. However, as Paul notes in this passage, God often works in ways that are considered foolish and incomprehensible by the world. Even today, His favorite instruments are often the "nobodies" that the world overlooks!

● How have you typically viewed the twelve disciples in the past? How does Jesus' choice of these very ordinary men to be His disciples encourage you?

_____

_____

_____

_____

_____

● Use the following scale to indicate how responsive you have been to the Lord's call on your life. In what ways might your response have been affected by opinions of others about you? In what ways has your response been affected by your own self-perceptions?

1	2	3	4	5	6	7	8	9	10

[very resistant]   [immediate and eager]

_____

_____

_____

_____

_____

_____

● Where has God surprised you most in His calling on your life? What is one way that He might be training you right now for the tasks that He has in store for you?

_____

_____

_____

_____

_____

_____

APPLYING TO YOUR LIFE

The twelve easy-to-overlook commoners whom Jesus called, trained, and sent out into the world as His disciples would never have been chosen by any other religious leader in history. Yet these are the men Jesus sought out for service in His kingdom! In the same way, know that God has not overlooked you. He has plans for *everyone* who says yes to Him. Given this, how are you preparing your heart, mind, and will for a lifetime in His service?

_____

_____

_____

_____

_____

_____

_____

_____

_____

CLOSING PRAYER

Lord Jesus, You haven't just called me to salvation; You've called me to a life of service to You. Thank You for seeing me even when others don't—for giving me real purpose in Your kingdom. Please open my eyes to the opportunities You're providing to share Your love and truth with others. And help me to look to You for the courage, the wisdom, and the responsiveness I need to carry out Your mission in this world. In Your powerful name. Amen.

Notes

1. Two disciples of John the Baptist are mentioned in John 1:35–42 as becoming disciples of Jesus, but only Andrew is named in the text (see verse 40). Some believe the other disciple was John, who is often unnamed in the Gospel (see 13:23), while some believe it was Philip (based on 1:43).
2. John MacArthur, author and general editor, *The MacArthur Study Bible* (Nashville, TN: Thomas Nelson, 1997), note on John 1:29.
3. MacArthur, *The MacArthur Study Bible*, note on Matthew 17:20.
4. John MacArthur, *Twelve Ordinary Men* (Nashville, TN: Thomas Nelson, 2002), 22.

LESSON 2

PETER

THE UNLIKELY LEADER

"And I also say to you that you are Peter, and on this rock I will build My church, and the gates of Hades shall not prevail against it. And I will give you the keys of the kingdom of heaven, and whatever you bind on earth will be bound in heaven, and whatever you loose on earth will be loosed in heaven."

MATTHEW 16:18-19

When you read the stories of the twelve disciples in the Gospels, you quickly realize they were an amazingly varied group. Their personalities and interests swept the spectrum. Perhaps there is no greater example of this than the disciple Peter. He stands out from the rest as having an aggressive, bold, and outspoken personality—one that often led to him revving his mouth while his brain was in neutral. We can, in fact, think of Peter as the disciple with the foot-shaped mouth. Yet, even with his tendency to be outspoken, Jesus saw great potential in him.

In the four biblical lists of the disciples (Matthew 10:2–4; Mark 3:16–19; Luke 6:13–16; Acts 1:13), Peter is always listed first, which indicates that he was the leader and spokesman for the whole company. In all four lists, the disciples are then arranged in three groups of four. Group one always has Peter at the head of the list, and that group includes Andrew, James, and John. Group two always features Philip first and includes Bartholomew, Matthew, and Thomas. Group three is always led by James the son of Alphaeus, and it includes Simon the Zealot, Judas the son of James, and Judas Iscariot (though he is omitted in the list in Acts).

Peter, this disciple with the foot-shaped mouth, was born Simon Bar-Jonah (meaning Simon, son of Jonah). He first appears in the Gospels when "Jesus, walking by the Sea of Galilee, saw two brothers, Simon called Peter, and Andrew his brother, casting a net into the sea; for they were fishermen" (Matthew 4:18). It was Jesus who later gave him the nickname Peter, which in the original Greek means "rock" or "stone." Certainly, a name like "Rock" would remind a person with an impetuous personality to remember who he *should* be in his best moments. It would also remind him how Jesus had discipled him to behave and act—a reminder that Peter would need later when he sinned by denying Christ.

The name would also help Peter after Jesus forgave him and gave him a mission. In fact, after Peter was forgiven, he would never look back. Ultimately, the record in the Gospels and book of Acts reveals that Jesus molded Simon Peter's strong personality into a rocklike leader, the greatest preacher among the apostles, and the dominant figure when the church was born. Peter's story serves as a great example for us today, for Jesus is still shaping the personality, character, and gifts of His disciples—and still giving them a new identity in Him.

STARTING OUT

Whether you know a little or a lot about the disciple Peter, what do you hope will happen as you learn about his life in this lesson?

_____

_____

_____

_____

_____

EXPLORING THE STORY

There is a long-standing debate about whether leaders are born or made. Peter is a strong argument for the belief that leaders are born with innate gifts but must also be properly shaped into true leaders. In this section, you will explore stories from the Gospels about how Jesus enacted this particular kind of "shaping" process in Peter's life.

The Raw Material of a Leader

Peter had several God-given qualities of leadership that were woven into the fabric of his personality from the very beginning. These rather obvious features in his natural disposition were not characteristics that could be developed merely by training. These three innate features of Peter's temperament were *inquisitiveness*, *initiative*, and *involvement*.

Inquisitiveness can be defined as "a strong interest in learning about many different things."[1] People who are inquisitive ask lots of questions to satisfy their curiosity. This is a necessary trait for a leader to possess, as those who are content with remaining ignorant about what they don't understand, complacent about what they haven't analyzed, and comfortable living with problems they have not solved do not make good leaders. Peter was inquisitive—he was genuinely hungry to gain knowledge from Christ and willing to ask the questions to get it.

THE LEADER OF THE APOSTLES

We know Peter was the leader of the apostles—and not only from the fact that his name heads every list of the Twelve. We also have the statement of Matthew 10:2: "Now the names of the twelve apostles are these: first, Simon, who is called Peter." The word translated *first* in that verse is the Greek term *protos*. It doesn't refer to the first in a list; it speaks of the chief, the leader of the group. Peter's leadership is further evident in the way he normally acts as spokesman for the whole group. He is always in the foreground, taking the lead. He seems to have had a naturally dominant personality, and the Lord put it to good use among the Twelve.[2]

Initiative can be defined as "the power of opportunity to do something before others do."[3] Those who demonstrate initiative have the drive, ambition, and energy to make things happen. This is obviously a crucial trait for leaders to possess, as they are the ones who blaze the trail for others, casting the vision for those who follow behind them. Peter took initiative—he was often not only the first to ask questions but also the first to answer those posed by Jesus. Peter was a man who seized the moment and charged ahead.

Involvement can be defined as "the act or process of taking part in something."[4] People who are involved always want to be right in the middle of the action. They do not sit in the background telling everyone else what to do while they live comfortably away from the fray. Rather, they go through life with a cloud of dust around them—an essential characteristic for all leaders to have. Peter was certainly involved in what was happening around him. In fact, he often jumped ahead of the other disciples without first thinking through his actions!

● Read Matthew 19:23–30. Inquisitiveness is the quality of being curious and eager to learn. What are some signs of Peter's natural inquisitiveness that you find in this passage?

_____

_____

_____

_____

_____

● Read Matthew 16:13–20. Initiative is the quality of assessing a situation and taking action. What are some signs of Peter's natural initiative that you find in this passage?

_____

_____

_____

_____

_____

_____

- Read Matthew 14:22–30. Involvement is the quality of wanting to be in the middle of the action. What are some signs of Peter's natural involvement that you find in this passage?

  _____

  _____

  _____

  _____

  _____

  _____

- Overall, what do you notice about Peter's personality in these passages? What are some traits of Peter's natural personality that you also possess?

  _____

  _____

  _____

  _____

  _____

The Experiences That Shape a Leader

It wasn't enough for Peter to just possess innate abilities of leadership. Those rough qualities alone would not make him into the kind of leader Jesus wanted him to be. So, for three years, the Lord took Peter through tests and trials to give him a *lifetime* of the kind of experiences that every true leader must endure. Peter learned at least three things through this process.

First, Peter discovered that *defeat and humiliation* often follow on the heels of victory. In a story told in Matthew 16:13–20, Jesus commended Peter and called him blessed for his response that Jesus was "the Christ, the Son of the living God." Jesus said, "On this rock I will build My church." This was a great victory for Peter. However, a few verses later, we find Peter rebuking Jesus for saying that He must suffer and die. Jesus then said to Peter, "Get behind Me, Satan! You are an offense to Me, for you are not mindful of the things of God, but the things of men" (verse 23). This was a crushing defeat and humiliation for Peter as a leader.

"GET BEHIND ME, SATAN!"

The harshness of this rebuke in Matthew 16:23 contrasts sharply with Jesus' words of commendation to Peter in verses 17–19. Jesus suggests that Peter is being a mouthpiece for Satan. Jesus' death is part of God's sovereign plan (see Acts 2:23; 4:27–28). "It pleased the LORD to bruise Him" (Isaiah 53:10). Christ came with the express purpose of dying as an atonement for sin (see John 12:27), and those who thwart His mission are doing Satan's work.[5]

Second, Peter learned that he was *not as strong on his own* as he thought. Peter declared to Jesus, in front of all the disciples, "Even if all are made to stumble because of You, I will never be made to stumble" (Matthew 26:33). Peter was confident in his strength to remain faithful to Christ no matter what happened. However, again just a few verses later, we find Peter denying that he even knew Jesus—just as the Lord said that he would. When the rooster crowed, Peter recognized that he was not as strong or secure as he had thought.

Third, Peter learned that Jesus *could still use him in spite of his failings*. The days following Jesus' resurrection found Peter and a few of the disciples back to fishing on the Sea of Galilee. Jesus met them there . . . and even cooked breakfast for the men. It was then that Jesus restored Peter and revealed that He still had great plans for him. Peter was to feed and tend to His sheep (see John 21:1–25). Failure would not define Peter as a leader.

- Read 2 Samuel 11:1–27. Peter was not the only leader in the Bible to experience defeat after victory. These events in this passage occur right after King David won a great battle against the Ammonites and Syrians. What defeat did he experience in this story?

_____

_____

_____

_____

_____

● Read 1 Corinthians 10:12–13. What warning does Paul offer? How did the truth of these words play out in the events leading up to Peter's denial?

_____

_____

_____

_____

_____

● Read 1 Peter 5:5–6. What did Peter learn from his failure?

_____

_____

_____

_____

● Overall, what did Peter learn from the difficult life experiences he endured? What are some important truths you have learned about yourself because of your life experiences?

_____

_____

_____

_____

The Qualities That Define a Leader

The final element needed for Peter to become an effective leader was the right *character*. Jesus understood that people would not respect and trust Peter—and thus not follow him—if he lacked character. So Jesus closely associated Himself with Peter and demonstrated through His life three character traits He wanted him to have: *submission, restraint,* and *humility*.

SUBMITTING TO GOD

"Therefore submit to God" (James 4:7). The Greek word for *submit* literally means "to line up under." The word was a military term used of soldiers under the authority of their commander. In the New Testament, it describes Jesus' submission to His parents' authority (see Luke 2:51), submission to human government (see Romans 13:1), the church's submission to Christ (see Ephesians 5:24), and servants' submission to their masters (see Titus 2:9; 1 Peter 2:18). James used the word to describe a willing, conscious submission to God's authority as sovereign ruler of the universe. A truly humble person will give his allegiance to God, obey His commands, and follow His leadership (see Matthew 10:38).[6]

Submission can be defined as "the act of yielding or surrendering . . . to another for a decision or consideration."[7] At first this might seem to be an odd quality for a leader to possess, as the general assumption is that leaders are the ones in charge and other people submit to them. However, true leaders provide an example of submission to their followers through the way they submit to the Lord and those in authority over them. Peter learned the importance of *submission* in a leader by submitting to Christ—the one in authority over him.

Restraint can be described as "the ability to control or moderate one's impulses and passions."[8] Self-control, discipline, moderation, and reserve are not always qualities that come naturally to those who live at the head of the pack— which is why anger is such a common and serious problem among leaders today. Peter certainly had his hotheaded moments. Jesus had to *constantly* teach him the value of restraint so he would become an effective leader.

Humility can be defined as "the attitude that you have no special importance that makes you better than others."[9] Leaders are often tempted by pride. In fact, one could say the besetting sin of leadership is the tendency for leaders to think more highly of themselves than they should. As noted previously, Peter had tremendous confidence in his own strength of will, which often got him into trouble. So Jesus allowed Peter to go through experiences that took him down a peg in the estimation of himself. In this way, Jesus taught Peter humility.

● Read Matthew 17:24–27. Peter evidently was wondering whether Jesus was morally obliged, as the Son of God, to pay for the upkeep of the temple like any mere human. What lesson did Jesus teach Peter in this case about submission to human authorities?

_____

_____

_____

_____

_____

_____

● Read John 18:1–11. This story relates what happened when Jesus was arrested. How did Peter fail to demonstrate the quality of restraint in this episode?

_____

_____

_____

_____

_____

_____

● Read Luke 22:31–34, 54–62. This is the account of Peter's denial of Christ as told by Luke. What are signs in this passage that Peter was prideful? How did he learn humility?

_____

_____

_____

_____

_____

_____

● Overall, why was it necessary for Peter to learn these character traits? What are some other character traits you think a good leader needs to have?

_____

_____

_____

_____

_____

_____

Considering Your Story

Read John 13:1–17. This story reveals one more quality of a good leader that Jesus modeled for Peter: *love*. All the disciples struggled with learning that true spiritual leadership meant loving service to one another. So Jesus demonstrated this to them by washing their dusty feet.

● Notice Peter's initial refusal to have his feet washed, followed by his insistence that he be entirely bathed. How would you react if Jesus said that He wanted to wash *your* feet?

_____

_____

_____

_____

_____

● When have you performed a lowly act of service like Jesus did for the disciples? What did you learn about loving others through the experience?

_____

_____

_____

_____

_____

- Although Peter denied Jesus, the Lord forgave, restored, and empowered him. The book of Acts reveals that Peter went on to serve as an integral leader (a rock) in the early church. As you reflect on this, circle the qualities below that you currently have or would like to have. Underline the qualities that you most want to be present in your life.

Inquisitiveness	Initiative	Involvement
Courage	Humility	Compassion
Submission	Restraint	Love

APPLYING TO YOUR LIFE

Although we think of the disciples as extraordinary, they were just ordinary men who followed the Savior. How would you like Jesus to shape and form your ordinary life as you follow Him? What would you like Him to teach you today?

_____

_____

_____

_____

_____

_____

_____

_____

CLOSING PRAYER

Jesus, Peter got it right and got it wrong on the same day. I can relate. Somehow, I've allowed myself to believe that the life You have for me only includes wonderful plans. If God's will for Your life included a cross, should I expect any less? Help me today to expect disappointment and difficulty and to prepare for them with Your Spirit's help. In our Lord Jesus' name. Amen.

Notes

1. "Inquisitiveness," *Oxford Learner's Dictionary*, https://www.oxfordlearnersdictionaries.com/us/definition/english/inquisitiveness.
2. John MacArthur, *Twelve Ordinary Men* (Nashville, TN: Thomas Nelson, 2002), 38.
3. "Initiative," *Merriam-Webster's Dictionary*, https://www.merriam-webster.com/dictionary/initiative.
4. "Involvement," *Cambridge Dictionary*, https://dictionary.cambridge.org/us/dictionary/english/involvement.
5. John MacArthur, author and general editor, *The MacArthur Study Bible* (Nashville, TN: Thomas Nelson, 1997), note on Matthew 16:23.
6. MacArthur, *The MacArthur Study Bible*, note on James 4:7.
7. "Submission," *Collins Dictionary*, https://www.collinsdictionary.com/us/dictionary/english/submission.
8. "Restraint," *Collins Dictionary*, https://www.collinsdictionary.com/us/dictionary/english/restraint.
9. "Humility," *Collins Dictionary*, https://dictionary.cambridge.org/us/dictionary/english/humility.

LESSON 3

ANDREW

THE APOSTLE OF SMALL THINGS

As He walked by the Sea of Galilee, He saw Simon and Andrew his brother casting a net into the sea; for they were fishermen.

MARK 1:16

It can be hard to live in the shadow of a brother of sister who excels at something. Perhaps you had a brother growing up who received a lot of attention for how good he was at academics. Or maybe you had a sister who always made the varsity team and stood out in athletics. Or maybe your older brother or sister was just more popular than you were at school.

The disciple Andrew—at least in the Gospel accounts—appears to have lived in the shadow of Peter, his better-known brother. Even though he was likely the first disciple to be called (see John 1:35–40) and was included in the lead group (see Mark 1:16–20; Matthew 4:18–22), he did not take part in several of the important events where Peter, James, and John were with Jesus (see Matthew 17:1;

Mark 5:37; 14:33). In fact, many of the verses that name Andrew add that he was Peter's brother, as if that is what made him significant!

We would expect in a situation like this for there to be resentment, sibling rivalry, and even estrangement in the relationship. However, in Andrew's case, we find no evidence in the Gospels that this ever occurred. Andrew and Peter appear to have been lifelong companions with James and John, the other set of fishermen brothers in Capernaum who would become Jesus' disciples. Andrew would have known about Peter's tendency to domineer, yet there is no sign of hesitation on his part when he introduced Peter to Jesus.

As a group, Peter, Andrew, James, and John exercised a sort of collective leadership over the other disciples. Yet of the four in the inner circle, Andrew was the least conspicuous. Apart from the places where all twelve disciples are listed, Andrew's name appears only nine times . . . and most of those references mention him in passing. Nonetheless, almost everything we read in the Bible where Andrew is mentioned reveals that he had the right heart for ministry. He did not seek to be the center of attention. He did not resent those who labored in the limelight. He was evidently pleased to do what he could with the gifts and calling God had bestowed on him. He was an effective leader who never took the spotlight.

In fact, Andrew might just be a *better* model for most church leaders today. Few of us will get the attention in ministry that Peter received. Most of us will minister in relative obscurity just like Andrew. This is why his story can be such an encouragement to us.

STARTING OUT

Think of a time when you lived in someone else's shadow. How positive or negative was that experience for you? How did you generally feel toward the person who got the attention?

_____

_____

_____

_____

_____

_____

EXPLORING THE STORY

Even though Andrew seemed content to play more of an unsung role among Jesus' disciples—and even though he is not mentioned as frequently as Peter, James, and John—we learn a lot about his character when he *is* mentioned in the Bible. In particular, what we find is that Andrew saw the value of *individual people*, of *insignificant gifts*, and of *inconspicuous service*. In this section, you will explore why these same values are important for Jesus' disciples today.

Value of Individual People

Both Andrew and his brother Peter desired for people to come to faith in Christ. We see this is true of Peter when he preached a sermon on the Day of Pentecost and about three thousand people joined the church (see Acts 2:14–41). There is no similar story of Andrew preaching a sermon like this that stirred the masses. However, what we do find Andrew doing is bringing *individual people* to Jesus. Andrew appreciated the value of a single soul.

Remember, the first time we encounter Andrew, he was a follower of John the Baptist. However, when Andrew saw his teacher look at Jesus and say, "Behold! The Lamb of God who takes away the sin of the world!" (John 1:29), he started following Jesus. Andrew and another unnamed disciple went to where Jesus was staying and remained with Him that day. Immediately after, Andrew found Peter and introduced him to Jesus (see verses 37–42).

FOLLOWING AFTER JESUS

"The two disciples heard him speak, and they followed Jesus" (John 1:37). The "following" here does not necessarily mean that these two men became permanent disciples at this time. The implication may be that they went after Jesus to examine Him more closely because of John's testimony. This event constituted a preliminary exposure of John the Baptist's disciples to Jesus. They eventually dedicated their lives to Him as true disciples when Jesus called them to permanent service after these events (see Matthew 4:18–22; 9:9; Mark 1:16–20).[1]

This incident set the tone for Andrew's style of ministry. A few chapters later in John, we read of Jesus' miraculous feeding of the five thousand. In the accounts of this story told in the other Gospels, the disciples were distressed in not knowing where they would get food for the crowd. When Jesus told the disciples to give them something to eat, they all complained that such a feat was impossible, for all they had were five loaves of bread and two fish (see Matthew 14:13–17; Mark 6:30–38; Luke 9:10–14). However, John adds the detail it was *Andrew* who brought the boy with the five loaves and two fish to Jesus (see John 6:4–9). Andrew alone saw the value in bringing this one individual—a boy—to his Master.

One other story told in John illustrates this character trait of Andrew. After Jesus' triumphal entry into Jerusalem, "certain Greeks" who were in the city to celebrate Passover asked to see Jesus (John 12:20). These were probably Gentiles who knew of Jesus' reputation and wanted to meet Him. They first went to Philip, who told Andrew about them (see verses 21–22). Why didn't Philip just directly ask Jesus? We don't know the reason. What we *do* know is that Philip understood Andrew could introduce such individuals to Jesus. Andrew understood that Jesus wanted to meet anyone who wanted to meet Him (see 6:37).

Andrew's example is important for us because most people do not come to Christ as an immediate response to a sermon they heard but because of a person who influenced them. Far too many Christians today believe they are not equipped for evangelism because they can't speak in front of groups or don't have leadership gifts. However, the truth is that all of us, like Andrew, can befriend just one person and influence him or her to follow Jesus.

● Read John 1:40–42. What does Andrew's unhesitating desire to bring his more domineering brother to Jesus say about his perspective and priorities?

_____

_____

_____

_____

_____

_____

_____

- Read Luke 15:4–7. Andrew appreciated the value of a single soul. What stands out in this parable about the value Jesus ascribes to one lost individual?

  _____

  _____

  _____

  _____

  _____

- Read John 4:39–42. Jesus went out of his way to meet one individual person—a Samaritan woman—at a well. What was the outcome of this meeting?

  _____

  _____

  _____

  _____

  _____

- What do you learn about evangelism through Andrew's example? What is one thing that God has specifically done through the influence of another person in your life?

  _____

  _____

  _____

  _____

  _____

Value of Insignificant Gifts

When Jesus was in Jerusalem the week before His death, He went to the place where offerings were made at the temple. Sitting there, He watched wealthy people cast large amounts of money into the treasury box. But what caught His attention was a poor widow who put in just two small copper coins. Calling His disciples, He said, "Assuredly, I say to you that this poor widow has put in more than all those who have given to the treasury; for they all put in out of their abundance, but she out of her poverty put in all that she had" (Mark 12:43–44).

THE WIDOW'S MITES

"He saw also a certain poor widow putting in two mites" (Luke 21:2). Thirteen chests with funnel-shaped openings stood in the court of the women in the temple. Each was labeled for a specific use, and donations were given accordingly. The Greek expression for "poor widow" signifies the woman was living in extreme poverty. She was desperately poor and more fit to be a recipient of charity than a donor. The *mite* was the smallest copper coin in use in Palestine, worth about one-eighth of a cent, but representing all on which this woman had to live.[2]

Andrew could accept the truth of this statement because he appreciated the value of seemingly insignificant gifts. Consider the story of the feeding of the five thousand that we just examined. In each of the Gospels, Jesus withdrew from the crowds to be alone with His disciples, but the clamoring multitudes tracked Him down. As the day grew late and it was nearing time to eat, Jesus decided to teach His disciples a lesson about God's provision. So He said, "Where shall we buy bread, that these [people] may eat?" (John 6:5).

Philip responded, "Two hundred denarii worth of bread is not sufficient for them, that every one of them may have a little" (verse 7).[3] Philip was the one who spoke up, but it is evident *all* the disciples were stymied as to how they could feed such a crowd. Again, Andrew was the only disciple who came up with any kind of solution. Certainly, he knew the boy's five barley loaves and two small fish could not feed five thousand people. But, in his typical fashion, he saw the merit in bringing the boy and his lunch to Jesus.

Jesus had commanded the disciples to feed the people. Andrew somehow understood that He would not issue such a command without making it possible for them to obey. We immediately see the result of Andrew's simple act of faith. "Jesus took the loaves, and when He had given thanks He distributed them to the disciples, and the disciples to those sitting down; and likewise of the fish, as much as they wanted" (verse 11). When the disciples gathered up the leftovers, what didn't get eaten of the five barley loves "filled twelve baskets" (verse 13).

It is amazing that something so little could be used to accomplish something so great. No gift is ever insignificant when it is in Jesus' hands. Andrew seemed instinctively to know this. He knew that he was not wasting Jesus' time by bringing such a paltry gift. He recognized it is not the greatness of the gift that counts but the greatness of the God to whom it is given.

- Read Luke 21:1–4. Where do people tend to go wrong in their measure of a gift's significance? How would you summarize Jesus' perspective of the woman's gift?

  _____
  _____
  _____
  _____
  _____

- Read John 6:5–9. What did Andrew recognize about the gift of the loaves and fish that he brought to Jesus? Why do you think he decided to bring them to Jesus regardless?

  _____
  _____
  _____
  _____
  _____

- Read 1 Timothy 4:12–14. What is Paul's advice to Timothy about using his gifts? Why might Timothy have been hesitant to use them in the church?

  _____
  _____
  _____
  _____
  _____
  _____

● What are some of the gifts you believe God has given to you? What is your attitude toward those gifts—and how are you using them for His kingdom?

_____

_____

_____

_____

_____

Value of Inconspicuous Service

Jesus said to His followers, "If you lend to those from whom you hope to receive back, what credit is that to you? For even sinners lend to sinners to receive as much back. But love your enemies, do good, and lend, hoping for nothing in return; and your reward will be great, and you will be sons of the Most High. For He is kind to the unthankful and evil" (Luke 6:34–35).

Some people won't play in the band unless they can hit the bass drum. They want their actions to be seen and heard by all. Peter had this tendency, as did James and John. Andrew, however, was one of those rare individuals who did not mind playing a supporting role as long as the work was being done. He labored quietly in humble places, "not with eyeservice, as men-pleasers, but as bond-servants of Christ, doing the will of God from the heart, with goodwill doing service, as to the Lord, and not to men" (Ephesians 6:6–7).

The Bible does not reveal what happened to Andrew after the Day of Pentecost. Luke states that he waited in Jerusalem with the other disciples for the coming of the Holy Spirit (see Acts 1:13), but after that there is no further mention of him. Whatever role Andrew played in the early church, as far as the book of Acts is concerned, happened behind the scenes. However, we do have early church traditions (history not in the Bible but passed down through the church community) that suggest Andrew took the gospel north.

Eusebius, a church historian who lived in the fourth century, wrote that Andrew preached in Scythia along the northern coast of the Black Sea.[4] He is believed to have been crucified in the city of Patras in Achaea, near Athens. One account says that he led the wife of a provincial Roman governor to Christ, which infuriated her husband. When she refused to recant, the governor had Andrew crucified (tradition states on an X-shaped cross).

ANDREW'S LEGACY

As far as we know, the disciple Andrew never preached to multitudes or founded any churches. He never wrote an epistle. He isn't mentioned in the book of Acts or any of the epistles. Andrew is more a silhouette than a portrait on the pages of Scripture. After a lifetime of ministry in the shadow of his more famous brother and in the service of His Lord, he then met a similar fate as theirs, remaining faithful and still endeavoring to bring people to Christ right to the end. Was he slighted? No. He was privileged. He was the first to hear that Jesus was the Lamb of God. He was the first to follow Christ. He was part of the inner circle, given intimate access to Christ. Best of all, he had a whole lifetime of privilege, doing exactly what he loved best: introducing individuals to the Lord.[5]

By most accounts, Andrew hung there for two days, exhorting passersby to turn to Jesus for salvation. If these stories are true, it means that after a lifetime of ministry in the shadow of his more famous brother and in the service of His Lord, he met a similar fate as theirs, remaining faithful and still endeavoring to bring people to Christ up until the end.

Andrew's example shows us the value of inconspicuous service. While his acts for God's kingdom might not have received the same attention as other disciples, they were not overlooked by Him. In fact, the Bible says his name will be inscribed, along with the names of the other disciples, on the foundations of the New Jerusalem (see Revelation 21:14).

● Read Proverbs 22:1; Matthew 23:11–12; and Mark 9:35. What do these passages from Scripture say about seeking prominence? Why are these cautions so important for Christians today?

_____

_____

_____

_____

_____

- Read Matthew 5:14–16. What does it mean to be "the light of the world" for Christ? What is ultimately the purpose of being a light and letting others see our good works?

  _____

  _____

  _____

  _____

- Read 1 Corinthians 3:3b–7. Based on Paul's words and Andrew's example, how would you describe the spirit toward servanthood that a disciple of Christ should have?

  _____

  _____

  _____

  _____

  _____

- How would you describe your attitude when it comes to serving quietly for God? How have you seen God reward your acts of inconspicuous service?

  _____

  _____

  _____

  _____

CONSIDERING YOUR STORY

Read 2 Timothy 4:1–2. Even though Andrew could be considered "the apostle of small things," he did big things for God when it came to bringing people to Jesus. He was obviously poised and comfortable introducing people to Christ, because he did it often and he knew Jesus well.

- Use the following scale to indicate your comfort level in bringing others to Jesus.

  O——O——O——O——O——O——O——O——O——O

  1   2   3   4   5   6   7   8   9   10

  [totally scared]   [always ready]

- How were you introduced to Jesus? How has that experience influenced your approach to bringing others to Him?

  _____

  _____

  _____

  _____

  _____

  _____

- Just like Andrew, being willing to bring people to Christ, sharing His priorities, and having a close relationship with Him will increase your confidence when it comes to engaging in spiritual conversations. What are some ways you can grow in each of these areas?

  Being more willing to bring people to Jesus:

  Sharing Jesus' priorities for the lost:

35

> Developing a closer relationship with Jesus:

APPLYING TO YOUR LIFE

In ministry, it's often the little things that count—the individual people, the insignificant gifts, and the inconspicuous service. God delights to use such things because He is the great Multiplier. What seemingly inconsequential pursuit do you want to entrust to Him today?

_____

_____

_____

_____

_____

_____

_____

CLOSING PRAYER

Jesus, I sometimes don't have the right attitude when it comes to serving others. I pass up what seem to be lesser opportunities because they aren't as high-profile as what other Christians are doing. Or I look down on opportunities because they're not as significant as what I think I could be doing. I need more of Andrew's mindset, where I'm willing to serve rather than having my ego served. Thank You for Your patience as I learn to value what You value. Amen.

Notes

1. John MacArthur, author and general editor, *The MacArthur Study Bible* (Nashville, TN: Thomas Nelson, 1997), note on John 1:37.
2. MacArthur, *The MacArthur Study Bible*, note on Luke 21:1–2.
3. A denarius was often equal to a day's wage for a laborer (see Matthew 20:2).
4. Eusebius (c. 260–339 AD), *Church History* 3.1.
5. John MacArthur, *Twelve Ordinary Men* (Nashville, TN: Thomas Nelson, 2002), 74.

LESSON 4

JAMES

THE APOSTLE OF PASSION

James and John, the sons of Zebedee, came to Him, saying,
"Teacher . . . grant us that we may sit, one on Your right hand and
the other on Your left, in Your glory."

MARK 10:35, 37

Zeal can be defined as "eagerness and ardent interest in the pursuit of something."[1] People who possess zeal can be inspirational. They are so passionate about what they believe in and so committed to making it happen that others can't help but want to join the cause. Yet zeal has its downside as well. These two sides are illustrated in the life of James.

James is the least familiar to us of the three disciples in Jesus' inner circle. We have story after story about Peter. There are many references to John. But James never appears as a standalone character in the Gospels. He is always paired with his better-known brother, and there are few details provided in the Bible about his life and character.

From a human perspective, James would have been the logical choice to dominate the group. As a member of Jesus' inner circle, he had the special privilege of witnessing Jesus' power in raising a dead girl (see Mark 5:37), seeing Jesus' glory when He was transfigured (see Matthew 17:1), and going further into the garden of Gethsemane with his Master (see Mark 14:33). Yet in two lists of the disciples, his name comes after Peter's (see Mark 3:16–19; Acts 1:13). While he was likely a strong leader, he was probably second in influence after Peter.

This is strange, because James and John are often referred to as "the sons of Zebedee" (Mark 10:35), which indicates their father was a man of some importance. There is even evidence that his family's reputation stretched from Galilee to the high priest's household in Jerusalem. Given that James was the elder brother from this prominent family, it seems natural that he would be the chief disciple. In truth, this might be one of the reasons why there were disputes about "which of them should be considered the greatest" (Luke 22:24).

What we do know about James is that he had great *zeal*. He was a man of intense fervor and passion. In fact, Jesus gave James and John the nickname Boanerges, which means "Sons of Thunder" (Mark 3:17). This defines James's personality in vivid terms. While Andrew was quietly bringing people to Jesus, James was wishing he could call down fire from heaven and destroy whole villages of people (see Luke 9:54)! Yet, through God's grace, James was ultimately transformed into a man of God who became one of the leading apostles.

STARTING OUT

Think about some of the best qualities of a passionate person whom you have known. How have you seen that person use his or her fervor for godly purposes?

_____

_____

_____

_____

_____

_____

EXPLORING THE STORY

Zeal apart from knowledge can be damning (see Romans 10:2). Zeal without wisdom is dangerous. Zeal mixed with insensitivity is often cruel. James sometimes tended to let such misguided zeal get the better of him. However, by the end of his life, his passion—now under the control of the Holy Spirit—would be so instrumental in spreading the truth that it would arouse the wrath of the king of Judea. In this section, you will explore James's zeal toward *those who were inhospitable*, his zeal for *greatness*, and ultimately his zeal for *the gospel*.

Zeal Toward the Inhospitable

Jehu was a king of Israel in the Old Testament who said, "Come . . . see my zeal for the LORD" (2 Kings 10:16) and then annihilated the house of Ahab and swept away Baal worship from the land. Jehu's passion was out of control, and his zeal for the Lord was tainted with worldly ambition and bloodthirsty cruelty. The Bible sums up the rest of his life with this somber statement: "Jehu took no heed to walk in the law of the LORD God of Israel with all his heart; for he did not depart from the sins of Jeroboam, who had made Israel sin" (verse 31).

James's zeal was mixed with similar ambition and bloodthirsty tendencies—though in milder doses—and he may have been headed down a similar road when Jesus met him. Luke gives us our best glimpse as to why this might be the case. Jesus was headed to Jerusalem for the Passover, which He knew would culminate in His death, burial, and resurrection. In that day, Jews had no dealings with Samaritans (see John 4:9) and even deemed the entire region to be unclean. However, Jesus chose the direct route to Jerusalem through Samaria.

Jesus sent messengers to the villages ahead to arrange accommodations for Him and the sizable party that was traveling with Him. However, the Samaritans in the first village refused to receive Jesus (see Luke 9:51–53). The messengers were, in fact, refused *all* accommodations. This was certainly due to the fact that the Samaritans had a long-standing hatred of the Jews—and the Jews a long-standing hatred of them.

James and John were outraged at the rebuff. They turned to Jesus and said, "Lord, do You want us to command fire to come down from heaven and consume them, just as Elijah did?" (verse 54). The reference to Elijah is significant. Centuries before, in this same region, Elijah had called down fire from heaven to destroy the soldiers that King Ahaziah, the son of Ahab, had sent against him

THE SAMARITANS

These people were descendants of Jewish mixed marriages from the days of captivity. They had devised their own worship, a hybrid of Judaism and paganism, with a temple of their own on Mount Gerizim. They were considered unclean by the Jews and were so hated that most Jewish travelers from Galilee to Judah took the longer route east of the Jordan River to avoid traveling through Samaria.[2]

(see 2 Kings 1:9–12). James and John knew this Old Testament story. When they suggested calling down fire from heaven as a fitting response to the Samaritans' inhospitality, they were probably thinking they stood on solid precedent.

But Jesus set a new precedent for them to follow. He taught James and his brother that *loving-kindness* and *mercy* were virtues to be cultivated as much as (and sometimes more than) righteous indignation and fiery zeal. He said, "The Son of Man did not come to destroy men's lives but to save them" (Luke 9:56), and then went to another village. The detour was a little inconvenient perhaps—but far better than what James and John were proposing!

A few years after this, Philip the deacon (not the apostle) preached in Samaria, and many people came to faith in Jesus (see Acts 8:5–8, 12–13). Undoubtedly, many of the people who were saved at this time were some of the same people whom Jesus spared when James asked to incinerate their village. We can be certain that even James himself rejoiced greatly in the salvation of so many individuals who once had dishonored Christ so flagrantly.

● Read the full story of Jehu's zeal in getting rid of Baal worship in 2 Kings 10:18–31. How would you describe his actions? How does the conclusion of this story reveal that Jehu was not truly passionate in following after God?

_____

_____

_____

_____

- Read Nehemiah 13:15–22. Nehemiah was one of many leaders in the Old Testament who was passionate about following after God. What actions did Nehemiah take in this passage? Why do you think this kind of zeal was approved by the Lord?

  _____
  _____
  _____
  _____
  _____

- Read John 12:46–47. A time is coming when Jesus will judge the world, but how did He describe His mission on earth to His followers? What impact do you think these words might have had on a zealous person like James?

  _____
  _____
  _____
  _____

- What do you learn about the dangers of zeal based on James's attitude toward the Samaritans? How has this kind of zeal caused problems in your life?

  _____
  _____
  _____
  _____

Zeal for Greatness

As Jesus was traveling the road to Jerusalem to celebrate His final Passover, He took His disciples aside and said, "The Son of Man will be betrayed to the chief priests and to the scribes; and they will condemn Him to death, and deliver Him to the Gentiles to mock and to scourge and to crucify. And the third day He will rise again" (Matthew 20:18–19). Jesus was about to lay down His life as a sacrifice for humanity's sin—the ultimate act of humility and mercy.

Immediately after this, the mother of James and John approached Jesus and made this astonishing and audacious request: "Grant that these two sons of mine may sit, one on Your right hand and the other on the left, in Your kingdom" (verse 21). Clearly, James and John had enlisted their mother's intercession in this matter. And, clearly, Jesus' message of humility and servanthood was not hitting the mark in their lives. The story reveals that James was fervent, passionate, and insensitive—but also ambitious and overconfident.

Where did James and his brother get the idea to make such a request? Most likely, the plan was hatched when they heard Jesus say, "Assuredly I say to you, that in the regeneration, when the Son of Man sits on the throne of His glory, you who have followed Me will also sit on twelve thrones, judging the twelve tribes of Israel" (Matthew 19:28). James and John were already in Jesus' intimate circle of three. So why *not* ask for this honor?

Jesus' reply subtly reminded them that suffering is the prelude to glory: "You do not know what you ask. Are you able to drink the cup that I am about to drink, and be baptized with the baptism that I am baptized with?" (Matthew 20:22). James and his brother—ever confident—answered, "We are able" (verse 22). So Jesus said to them, "You will indeed drink My cup, and be baptized with the baptism that I am baptized with; but to sit on My right hand and on My left is not Mine to give, but it is for those for whom it is prepared by My Father" (verse 23).

SALOME

By comparing Matthew 27:56 with Mark 16:1, we discover that the mother of James and John was named Salome. She was one of the "women who followed Jesus from Galilee, ministering to Him" (Matthew 27:55)—meaning that these women supplied financial support and probably helped prepare meals (see Luke 8:1–3). Because of the family's affluence, Salome would have been able to join her sons for extended periods of time, traveling with the company that followed Jesus everywhere and helping meet logistical, practical, and financial needs.[3]

Jesus had just explained to them that He was about to be crucified. He was now saying they would "drink the cup" He was about to drink and "be baptized" with the baptism He was about to receive. They did not understand in that moment what was stirring in the cup He was asking them to drink. They clearly did not understand what kind of baptism He meant.

James wanted power; Jesus gave him servanthood. He wanted a crown of glory; Jesus gave him a cup of suffering. He wanted a place of prominence; Jesus gave him a martyr's grave. James would become the first of the twelve disciples to be killed for his faith.

- Read Matthew 19:28–30. What promise did Jesus give to His disciples? What reminder did He give at the end of this passage about who is truly considered great in God's kingdom?

  _____

  _____

  _____

  _____

- Read Matthew 20:24–28. How did the other disciples react to the ambition of James and John? What reminder did Jesus again give to them all about greatness in God's kingdom?

  _____

  _____

  _____

  _____

- Read Luke 22:24–27. What was the nature of the disciples' dispute? What did Jesus say here about the connection between service and greatness?

  _____

  _____

  _____

  _____

● Why do you think Jesus had to remind James and the other disciples so often about the importance of humility and service? When have you needed this reminder from Christ in response to your own ambitions?

_____

_____

_____

_____

_____

_____

_____

_____

Zeal for the Gospel

There is one place in the Bible where James appears apart from his brother. As Luke records: "Now about that time Herod the king stretched out his hand to harass some from the church. Then he killed James the brother of John with the sword. And because he saw that it pleased the Jews, he proceeded further to seize Peter also" (Acts 12:1–3).

When Jesus was born, King Herod the Great issued a command to have "all the male children who were in Bethlehem and in all its districts" put to death (Matthew 2:16). Years later, his son, Herod Antipas, had John the Baptist killed (see Matthew 14:1–12) and Jesus put on trial (see Luke 23:6–12). Now, his nephew and successor, Herod Agrippa I, ordered the execution of James "with the sword," which means he was beheaded.

We don't know why this Herod was hostile to the church. Of course, his uncle had participated in the plot to kill Jesus, so the growth of the church would have been an embarrassment to his dynasty (see Acts 4:27). Persecutions led by the Jewish religious leaders had broken out against followers of Jesus (see 8:1), so Herod likely wanted to use the tensions this generated between the two groups to his political advantage. Herod first harassed members of the church, and then murdered James, one of Jesus' own disciples. When Herod saw how this pleased the Jewish leaders, he decided to target Peter as well.

It is significant that James was the first of the twelve disciples to be killed—the only apostle whose death in actually recorded in the New Testament. Clearly,

HEROD AGRIPPA I

Herod Agrippa I, the grandson of Herod the Great, reigned from AD 37 to 44. History reports that he ran up numerous debts in Rome and fled to Palestine. Imprisoned by Emperor Tiberius after some careless comments, he eventually was released following Tiberius's death and was made ruler of northern Palestine, to which Judea and Samaria were added in AD 41. As a hedge against his shaky relationship with Rome, he curried favor with the Jews by persecuting Christians.[4]

James was still a man of passion! This Son of Thunder had now been mentored by Christ, empowered by the Holy Spirit, and shaped by those means into a man whose zeal and ambition were useful instruments in the hands of God for spreading His kingdom. James had evidently learned to use those qualities for God's service rather than for his own self-promotion. His zeal for the gospel had become so great that when Herod decided it was time to stop the church, the disciple James was the first man whom he targeted to die a martyr's death.

This is bolstered by an account of James's execution from Clement of Alexandria as recorded by Eusebius: "The one who led James to the judgment-seat, when he saw him bearing his testimony, was moved, and confessed that he was himself also a Christian. They were both therefore . . . led away together; and on the way he begged James to forgive him. And [James], after considering a little, said, 'Peace be with thee,' and kissed him. And thus they were both beheaded at the same time."[5] James had learned to be more like Andrew, bringing people to Jesus instead of itching to execute divine judgment against them.

There is nothing inherently wrong with zeal. When Jesus made a whip and cleansed the temple, His disciples remembered that it had been written, "Zeal for Your house has eaten Me up" (John 2:17; see also Psalm 69:9). James, of all people, knew what it was to be "eaten up" with zeal for God. Much of what James saw Jesus do for the sake of righteousness likely stoked his zeal. James died in the place where he had always hoped to be (and where Jesus had trained him to be)—right on the front lines as the gospel advanced and the church grew.

● Read 1 Corinthians 9:16–18. How does Paul describe his zeal for the gospel? What does he consider to be his "reward" in preaching it?

_____

_____

_____

_____

● Read Philippians 1:12–14. Paul, like James, was imprisoned for proclaiming the gospel. What purpose did Paul see in the fact that he was in chains?

_____

_____

_____

_____

● Read Titus 2:11–14. What are some of the things followers of Jesus are to zealously pursue? Why are we commanded to be zealous for good works?

_____

_____

_____

_____

● Can you say that you are _zealous_ in sharing the gospel with the lost? What do you learn from James's example about the sacrifice and rewards that result from this kind of zeal?

_____

_____

_____

_____

CONSIDERING YOUR STORY

Read Galatians 5:22–26. Somewhere along the line, James learned to bridle his tongue, redirect his zeal, eliminate his thirst for revenge, and lose his selfish ambition. As a result of this, the Lord was able to use him to do a mighty work in the early church.

● In which areas have you seen the Lord humble you or temper your passions? What was an important lesson that God taught you about your zeal?

_____

_____

_____

_____

_____

● How has God's long-suffering with you directly impacted your patience and mercy toward others? How has walking in the Spirit helped you to keep from being self-centered?

_____

_____

_____

_____

● As you consider the life and transformation of James, which two or three fruit of the Spirit in your own life most need the Lord's pruning right now? Circle these below.

Love	Joy	Peace
Long-suffering	Kindness	Goodness
Faithfulness	Gentleness	Self-control

APPLYING TO YOUR LIFE

A fervent man like James would have likely caused his own ruin (and that of others) had he not submitted his passions to the Lord and undergone His "tempering" process. What does this tempering process look like in your life? How has God taught you mercy and grace?

_____

_____

_____

_____

_____

_____

_____

_____

_____

_____

_____

CLOSING PRAYER

Almighty God, I'm grateful that You have given me a passion for ministry and zeal for You. I also thank You for Your persistent grace in refining me where I need it. You never give up on me but correct me, instruct me, and—all the while—lovingly push me toward greater godliness and maturity. I pray that You will continue to temper my passions and ambitions so I'm doing the work You would have me doing, in the way You want it done. In Your glorious name. Amen.

Notes

1. "Zeal," *Merriam-Webster's Dictionary*, https://www.merriam-webster.com/dictionary/zeal.
2. John MacArthur, author and general editor, *The MacArthur Study Bible* (Nashville, TN: Thomas Nelson, 1997), note on Luke 9:52.
3. John MacArthur, *Twelve Ordinary Men* (Nashville, TN: Thomas Nelson, 2002), 90–91.
4. MacArthur, *The MacArthur Study Bible*, note on Acts 12:1.
5. Eusebius, *Ecclesiastical Church History*, 2.9.2–3.

LESSON 5

JOHN

THE APOSTLE OF LOVE

Then Peter, turning around, saw the disciple whom Jesus loved following,
who also had leaned on His breast at the supper, and . . .
seeing him, said to Jesus, "But Lord, what about this man?"

JOHN 21:20-21

The disciple John is familiar to us not only as the disciple "whom Jesus loved" (John 13:23) but also because of what the Bible reveals about him through his own writings. As the human author of a sizable portion of the New Testament—a Gospel, three epistles, and the book of Revelation—we have a real sense of who he was as both a person and a disciple of Christ. Yet, surprisingly, he wasn't one of the dominant ones in Jesus' inner circle . . . at least not while his older brother James and the outspoken Peter were around. John eventually did become a central figure in the early church, and he was loved by Christians as a spiritual father.

Today, when we think of John, we forget that he was one of the "Sons of Thunder" (Mark 3:17). We instead think of him as the wizened elder statesman of the faith who constantly wrote on the ideals of loving Christ and loving one another. We forget that, time and again, he was right there acting in concert with his brother James—zealous to call down fire from heaven against the Samaritans and elbowing for position in Jesus' future kingdom. His zeal and ambition mirrored that of his elder brother.

So, how did John become known as "the apostle of love"? Part of the answer comes from the fact that John wrote so frequently on the topic of love in the New Testament—emphasizing the Christian's love for Christ, Jesus' love for His church, and the love for one another that is supposed to be the hallmark of true believers. The greater reason, however, is far more personal. John *learned* love from the One who loved him the most. Once that love had sunk in, this once-tempestuous man was never the same.

Just as Peter was the opposite of a steady "Rock" when he first met Jesus, so the younger Son of Thunder appears to have been anything but a loving apostle in the beginning. Truth always remained his passion, and John often spoke in black-and-white terms—a teaching style he no doubt learned from Jesus. Yet it is also clear that John learned the quality of *love* from Jesus and came to understand the value of "speaking the truth in love" (Ephesians 4:15). The Lord matured him and, over time, he became the beloved leader of the first-century church.

Three years with Jesus began the process of transforming John from a self-centered fanatic into a mature man of balance. Three years with Jesus moved him toward becoming an apostle of love. Jesus gave him equilibrium at the very points where he was most imbalanced. This why today, John stands as one of the Bible's shining examples of what lifelong spiritual growth should look like in the life of every true follower of Christ.

THE DISCIPLE WHOM JESUS LOVED

While the synoptic Gospels identify John by name approximately twenty times (including parallels), he is not so directly mentioned in the Gospel of John. Instead, the author identifies himself simply as the disciple "whom Jesus loved" (13:23; 19:26; 20:2; 21:7, 20). John's deliberate avoidance of mentioning his own personal name reflects his humility and celebrates his relation to his Lord Jesus.[1]

STARTING OUT

Think of a leader you have known for years from work, within your family, in the church, or in your community. As you've watched that person age, how would you characterize his or her "trajectory"? Is this individual aging well like John or aging poorly? Explain your answer.

_____

_____

_____

_____

_____

_____

_____

_____

_____

EXPLORING THE STORY

John was as rugged as any of the other fisherman-disciples. He was also as self-centered, hot-headed, and zealous as any of his peers. In fact, in his younger years, it would be fair to say he was prone to extremes in his thinking and his reactions. Jesus had to temper John's thunderous personality by teaching him the balance between *truth and love, ambition and humility,* and *suffering and glory*. In this section, we will explore how John learned these lessons.

Balance Between Truth and Love

John grew to become a beloved spiritual father and tenderhearted representative of the gospel, but Jesus never tried to displace the apostle's fierce passion for truth. Rather, the Lord taught John to hold truth and love in balance. Even early on, John had a heart that seemed calibrated for truth. We see this in how quickly he followed Jesus. All he needed was confirmation that Jesus was indeed the Messiah, and he was all in (see John 1:35–37).

John's love for truth was also evident in the way he wrote. While John communicated to his audience in a warm, pastoral tone, his biblical messages aren't the first place we can turn for an encouraging word! True to his temperament, he thought and wrote in absolutes—to the extent that an undiscerning reader might think he was still an extremist. John wrote that people are either walking in the light or dwelling in darkness. They either receive Christ or reject Him. They either love or hate . . . no in-between. John made sure in his writings that nothing about God's truth was fuzzy to believers. Of all the New Testament authors, he is the most cut-and-dried, drawing clear and convicting lines.

At the same time, John lovingly addressed his epistles to "my little children" (1 John 2:1); "the elect lady and her children, whom I love in truth" (2 John 1); and "the beloved Gaius, whom I love in truth" (3 John 1). He urged his readers to "love one another" (2 John 5) and "walk according to [God's] commandments," for "this is love" (verse 6). He reminded them, "This is the message that you heard from the beginning, that we should love one another" (1 John 3:11), adding, "Let us not love in word or in tongue, but in deed and in truth" (verse 18).

In John's epistles, written from the perspective of a disciple who has matured in the faith, we find a *balance* between truth and love. However, this was not always the case in John's younger years. A prime example is found in a story told in Mark's Gospel. John, after taking part in a debate about who among the disciples would be the greatest (see 9:33–34), said to Jesus, "Teacher, we saw someone who does not follow us casting out demons in Your name, and we forbade him because he does not follow us" (verse 38).

This same episode is also recorded in Luke's Gospel, just before the account of James and John asking to call down fire to annihilate the Samaritan town. In both cases, John was displaying an appalling intolerance, elitism, and lack of genuine love for people. In the incident with the Samaritans, James and John showed a lack of love for unbelievers. Here, John was guilty of a similar kind of unloving spirit toward a fellow believer. In John's view, if someone did not "follow with us" (Luke 9:49), that person was against them. But in Jesus' view, "No one who works a miracle in My name can soon afterward speak evil of Me. For he who is not against us is on our side" (Mark 9:39–40).

It is interesting that John chose to confess this to Jesus at all. Perhaps the reason is because he felt convicted. John had just watched Jesus take a little child, set him in the midst of the disciples, and say, "Whoever receives one of these little children in My name receives Me; and whoever receives Me, receives not Me but Him who sent Me" (Mark 9:37). Perhaps John was realizing that his thinking and approach toward others left much to be desired.

A TRANSFORMATION

The fact that John made this confession was indicative of the transformation that was taking place in him. His conscience was bothering him. He was being tenderized. He had always been zealous and passionate for the truth, but now the Lord was teaching him to love. This is a major turning point in his life and thinking. He was beginning to understand the necessary equilibrium between love and truth.[2]

God's kingdom needs people who have courage, ambition, drive, passion, boldness, and a zeal for the truth. Yet balance is necessary. Anyone who longs to serve effectively for God must cultivate truth and love in equal proportions—loving as Jesus taught us to love.

- Read 1 John 3:4–9. John, of course, knew that believers do fall into sin at times (see John 1:8). So what is he saying here about sin and what it represents in a believer's life? What is the black-and-white truth about sin that John is illuminating for followers of Christ?

  _____

  _____

  _____

  _____

- Read 1 John 3:16–17. John, of course, knew that believers fail to love others at times. So what is he saying here about love and how it should be evident in a believer's life? What is the black-and-white truth about love that John is illuminating for followers of Christ?

  _____

  _____

  _____

  _____

- Read Luke 9:46–48. How might this lesson have prompted John to rethink whether he should have forbade the man from casting out demons in Jesus' name? What was Jesus teaching the disciples about loving one another?

  _____

  _____

  _____

  _____

- What do you learn about the importance of truth and love based on the stories you have read involving John? How well do you strike this balance in your interactions with people?

  _____

  _____

  _____

  _____

  _____

Balance Between Ambition and Humility

Most young people today have dreams and ambitions—and that is a good thing. John certainly did . . . and Jesus saw it as a good thing. In the Lord's eyes, the problem wasn't that John had dreams and goals but rather his *spirit* and *motives* behind those ambitions. In John's story, what we find early on in his life is that he was driven by selfishness, pride, and ego.

Ambition without humility is not only dangerous but also a sin. Humility is so important that Jesus reminded His disciples numerous times of its necessity in their zeal for ministry. One of those reminders was precipitated by the request from John and his brother to be seated next to Jesus in the coming kingdom. We looked at this story in the previous lesson as it was told in the Gospel of Matthew. Here, we will take a look at the story from Mark's Gospel.

In Mark's account, we find that James's and John's timing is ironic. They approached Jesus shortly after John had admonished the fellow believer (see Mark 9:38–41) *and* just a few verses after Jesus had said, "Many who are first will be last, and the last first" (10:31). Again, having ambition wasn't where James and

John went wrong. The brothers' error was in desiring the *position* more than they desired to be *worthy* of such a position. Coming as it did on the heels of so many admonitions from Jesus about humility, the brothers' request shows amazing audacity. It reveals how utterly devoid of true humility they were.

What follows in Mark's Gospel also reveals how devoid of humility *all* the disciples were, for "when the ten heard it, they began to be greatly displeased with James and John" (verse 41). The others were *displeased* because they also wanted positions of authority in Jesus' kingdom and were none too pleased when they saw John and James asserting themselves. The squabble prompted Jesus to remind them that the highest positions in His kingdom will be reserved for the humblest saints on earth (see verses 41–45).

John eventually did learn to balance his ambition with humility. In his Gospel, he never mentions his own name. Instead, he calls himself "the disciple whom Jesus loved" (John 13:23; 20:2; 21:7, 20). This isn't prideful John trying to lord his closeness to Jesus over the other disciples. Rather, this is mature John glorifying Jesus for having loved someone like him.

Jesus' example of love *and* humility had a humbling effect on John. In fact, it is only John's Gospel that details Jesus' ministry of washing the disciples' feet at the Last Supper. That the sinless Son of God would do such a thing the night before His death made a lasting impression on John, for the disciple lived what he learned from his Lord to his dying day.

HUMILITY

The term *humility* is not found in the Latin or Greek vocabularies of the first century. The Greek word frequently used for *humility* in the New Testament—*tapeinoó,* literally meaning "lowliness" (see Ephesians 4:2)—was apparently coined by Christians (perhaps even by the apostle Paul) to describe a quality for which no other word was available. Humility, the most foundational Christian virtue (see James 4:6), is the quality of character commanded in the first beatitude (see Matthew 5:3) and describes the noble grace of Christ (see Philippians 2:7–8).[3]

● Read John 13:3–17. Jesus not only taught His disciples about humility but also personally modeled it for them. What instructions did Jesus give to them at the end of this passage?

_____

_____

_____

_____

_____

● Read 1 John 3:1–3. Notice John's words about his readers. What do these expressions indicate about the transformation of his character?

_____

_____

_____

_____

● Read 3 John 9–10. What was it about Diotrephes that drew John's attention? Why do you think John was able to so clearly recognize this fault?

_____

_____

_____

_____

● Think about some of the ambitions you have and the skills you possess to achieve them. How do you balance these ambitions in your life with humility?

_____

_____

_____

_____

Balance Between Suffering and Glory

In John's younger years, he had a thirst for glory. He and his brother had gone so far as to assure Jesus they could drink His cup of suffering (see Mark 10:39). But when the moment of truth came the night before His crucifixion—surrounded by a crowd with swords and clubs and with Jesus' betrayer in their midst—what did John and the other disciples do? They abandoned their Savior, Teacher, and Lord in the hope of avoiding suffering (see 14:43–50).

John had seen Jesus' glory firsthand on the Mount of Transfiguration. He treasured Jesus' promise that he would share in that glory (see Matthew 19:28–29). John's desire was similar to that of the psalmist who wrote, "As for me, I will see Your face in righteousness; I shall be satisfied when I awake in Your likeness" (Psalm 17:15). A desire to participate in Jesus' glory is therefore fitting for every child of God. But Jesus was clear that those who desire to participate in His heavenly glory must also be willing to partake of earthly sufferings.

Paul wrote, "The Spirit Himself bears witness with our spirit that we are children of God, and if children, then heirs—heirs of God and joint heirs with Christ, if indeed we suffer with Him, that we may also be glorified together" (Romans 8:16–17). Suffering is the price of glory. The "chief seats" in God's kingdom are not the "cheap seats." There is a cost to pay.

John and James had been naïve in proclaiming they could drink of the cup Jesus would drink and be baptized with the baptism of suffering He would endure (see Mark 10:38–39). James was the first to realize what this actually meant when he was imprisoned by Herod and then sent to a martyr's death. But the rest of the disciples would follow. Tradition states that they all were martyred one by one, in the prime of life, in horrific ways. All of them, that is, except for John. He alone of the twelve disciples lived to an old age.

Yet this does not mean that John escaped suffering. Certainly, he bore the loss of his brother in a deeply personal way. He would have witnessed the other disciples being put to death one by one—suffering each loss of his friends and companions with renewed grief and pain. In some ways, that might have been the most painful suffering of all. Furthermore, early sources state that John became the pastor of the church that Paul had founded in Ephesus and then was exiled to a prison community on Patmos, located in the Aegean Sea.

This took place during a persecution of the church under the Emperor Domitian. There, on Patmos, John lived in a dank cave, slept on a rock slab, and endured cruel treatment with no access to his loved ones. It was just one more lesson in John's life about the balance between suffering and glory. Even so, the book that John penned on that remote island contains no hint of bitterness. Instead, he described himself to his fellow believers as "both your brother and companion in the tribulation and kingdom and patience of Jesus Christ" (Revelation 1:9).

How many of us would say the same? Only those who, like John, have the proper perspective of what is required in the here and now to receive future glory with Christ. As Peter wrote, "In this you greatly rejoice, though now for a little while, if need be, you have been grieved by various trials, that the genuineness of your faith, being much more precious than gold that perishes, though it is tested by fire, may be found to praise, honor, and glory at the revelation of Jesus Christ" (1 Peter 1:6–7). This is the balance between suffering and glory.

- Read Matthew 16:24–28. How does Jesus describe the cost of being His follower? What does He say is the reward for being faithful to Him?

  _____

  _____

  _____

  _____

  _____

  _____

- Read John 18:12–15. It is likely the reference to "another disciple" is John. What firsthand experience of suffering did John learn from Jesus in this scene? How do you think this event enabled John to understand the true cost of being a disciple of Christ?

  _____

  _____

  _____

  _____

  _____

  _____

- Read Philippians 3:8–11. Why was Paul willing to suffer "the loss of all things" in this world for the sake of Christ? What type of "fellowship" did Paul want to know?

  _____

  _____

  _____

  _____

- How do you respond to this idea that earthly suffering is the price of eternal glory? How could keeping your focus on the rewards that you will receive from Jesus in the life to come help you to deal with the pain and suffering that come in this present life?

  _____

  _____

  _____

  _____

Considering Your Story

Read John 19:25–27. Few who knew John in his early years would have thought of him as "the apostle of love." Yet this scene from the cross shows that John got the message. He learned Jesus' lessons so well that the Lord assigned him the care of His own mother.

- Jesus told Peter, "Feed My sheep" (John 21:17). He told John, "Take care of My mother." What would be your response if Jesus were to ask such a thing of you today?

  _____

  _____

  _____

  _____

● What are some practical ways that God's love has transformed your opinion of others? How has His love transformed your actions toward others?

_____

_____

_____

_____

_____

_____

_____

● John learned the importance of balance. Think about a task that you believe God has given you to do. What are the top three areas in which you need balance to accomplish that task?

Balance in the first area . . .

Balance in the second area . . .

Balance in the third area . . .

APPLYING TO YOUR LIFE

Jesus' love and the work of the Holy Spirit moved John from the far edges of zeal to spiritual maturity, steadiness, and love. What are some of the main takeaways that you have gained from John's example? What would you like God to help you understand about yourself?

_____

_____

_____

_____

_____

_____

CLOSING PRAYER

Lord, I can be quick to avoid pain, judge others, and feed my pride. I don't want those impulses to become ways of life. I want my legacy to be that of a loving servant-leader who stays in step with You. Some days I can see progress—I see You maturing me. Other days I get caught up in my own plans and schemes. Today, I have this one request: Cultivate Your desires in my life so that I am centered in Your will. In Your glorious name. Amen.

Notes

1. John MacArthur, author and general editor, *The MacArthur Study Bible* (Nashville, TN: Thomas Nelson, 1997), introduction to the Gospel of John.
2. John MacArthur, *Twelve Ordinary Men* (Nashville, TN: Thomas Nelson, 2002), 105.
3. MacArthur, *The MacArthur Study Bible*, note on Ephesians 4:2.

LESSON 6

PHILIP

THE BEAN COUNTER

Philip answered Him, "Two hundred denarii worth of bread is not sufficient for them, that every one of them may have a little."

JOHN 6:7

In the four biblical lists of the disciples, each arranged into three groups of four (Matthew 10:2–4; Mark 3:16–19; Luke 6:13–16; Acts 1:13), the fifth name is always Philip. This indicates Philip was the leader of the second group that included Bartholomew, Matthew, and Thomas. In the Gospels, he plays a bit of a minor role when compared to the men in the first group. Yet he is mentioned several times, so he emerges as a distinct individual in his own right.

Philip is a Greek name meaning "lover of horses" His Jewish name is never given. This could mean he came from a family of Hellenistic (Greek-influenced) Jews. The *disciple* Philip is not to be confused with the *deacon* Philip who preached in Samaria and led an Ethiopian eunuch to Christ (see Acts 6:5; 8:4–13, 26–40).

PHILIP THE DEACON

This Philip was one of seven men chosen to oversee the daily distribution of food in the church in response to a complaint by the Hellenists (Jews from the Diaspora) that their widows were being overlooked (see Acts 6:1–7). He is the first missionary named in Scripture and the first given the title "evangelist" (21:8).[1]

Philip the disciple was from Bethsaida, the hometown of Peter and Andrew (see John 1:44). Being God-fearing Jews, Philip likely knew the brothers from synagogue and, through them, knew their fishing partners, James and John. There is evidence that Philip was also a Galilean fisherman, for he accepted Peter's invitation (with Nathanael and Thomas) to go fishing after the resurrection (see John 21:2–3)

When we put these details together, we see the group of disciples were a close-knit bunch. Prior to answering Jesus' call, these seven men were likely already acquaintances, if not friends. Given this, it is rather surprising that Jesus would select more than *half* of His team from the same small region and business community. One would think that He would at least conduct a search throughout Judea for the gifted candidates. Instead, what we find is Jesus selecting a core group of rugged, working-class men with unremarkable resumés. All that Jesus required was availability—and Philip evidently fit that requirement.

All of the vignettes of Philip come from the Gospel of John—Matthew, Mark, and Luke give us no details about him. What we find in John's Gospel is that Philip is often paired with Nathanael, which likely means that the two were close comrades. Beyond this, we learn that Philip was unique among the disciples as a classic "operations person." He was the facts-and-figures guy, by the book and practically minded, rigidly adhering to protocols and procedures, and practical to the point of sometimes being a killjoy.

Philip was predisposed to be a pragmatist and a cynic—and sometimes a defeatist—rather than a visionary. Given this, he does not seem like the ideal candidate for a disciple. But Jesus had a different perspective. Philip was exactly the kind of person Jesus was seeking, for his weaknesses would serve as the perfect platform for displaying Christ's strength.

STARTING OUT

Describe the most classic "bean counter" you have known. Did you ever get to see the heart behind that person? If so, what were you surprised to discover?

_____

_____

_____

_____

_____

_____

EXPLORING THE STORY

Jesus drew the men He selected for His disciples to Himself, trained them, gifted them, and empowered them to serve Him. Maybe this is why He chose so many rugged fishermen—they were better suited to the task of operating in *His* power than a group of prodigies would have been trying to operate in their own talent. Still . . . what did He see in Philip? Based on clues we find in John, Philip was *awaiting the Messiah*, yet *hesitant and pessimistic*, and also *uncertain and indecisive* at times. You will explore each of these aspects of his character in this section.

Awaiting the Messiah

Philip appears in the opening chapter of John's Gospel. The day after the calling of Andrew, John, and Peter, "Jesus wanted to go to Galilee, and He found Philip and said to him, 'Follow Me'" (1:43). Notice the wording: "*He* found Philip" (emphasis added). This is the first time we read of Jesus seeking out one of His disciples. Of course, He sovereignly sought out and called the others, but this language regarding Philip's calling is unique. When the Lord found Philip, He found a disciple with an open heart who had been eagerly awaiting *Him*.

After meeting Jesus, Philip sought out his close companion, Nathanael, and said, "We have found Him of whom Moses in the law, and also the prophets, wrote—Jesus of Nazareth, the son of Joseph" (verse 45). Notice again the wording: "*We* have found Him" (emphasis added). In Philip's mind, *he* had found the Messiah rather than being found by Him. Clearly, both he and Nathanael had been studying the Old Testament. They were excitedly on the lookout for the Messiah. So when Jesus said, "Follow Me," it was all Philip needed. The search was over. His ears, his eyes, and his heart were already open and he was ready to follow.

Granted, Philip never expected a lowly carpenter's son from a small town (Nazareth in Galilee) to be the anointed One. Nevertheless, he received Jesus as the Messiah without hesitation, reluctance, or disbelief. "Come and see," he simply said when Nathanael expressed his doubts. Philip was like "a man in Jerusalem whose name was Simeon . . . waiting for the Consolation of Israel, and the Holy Spirit was upon him" (Luke 2:25).

Philip's receptivity must be highlighted in this case precisely because it was so out of character for him. His natural tendency was to hang back, hold off, ask tough questions—to not rush too quickly. In Philip's calling, though, we see his spiritual side shining through. The Lord had prepared his heart. By the time Jesus called Philip, he had already been drawn to Christ by the Father. As Jesus said, "All that the Father gives Me will come to Me" (John 6:37).

- Read John 1:10–13. Philip was one of those in Israel who chose to receive Jesus as the Messiah. What does this passage say that those who likewise receive Jesus become?

_____

_____

_____

_____

_____

_____

- Read John 6:41–44. What does Jesus say about God's role in bringing people to Him? What does this reveal about God's character and nature?

_____

_____

_____

_____

_____

_____

● Read 1 Corinthians 2:14–16. God had prepared Philip's heart to receive Jesus. According to the apostle Paul, how do we likewise prepare our hearts to receive the things of God?

_____

_____

_____

_____

_____

● What are some ways that you are actively seeking a relationship with Christ in your life? How have you witnessed God draw you to Himself?

_____

_____

_____

_____

_____

Hesitant and Pessimistic

Our next glimpse of Philip occurs at the miracle of the feeding of the five thousand. In this story, we witness Philip's inherent tendency to narrow in and calculate the reasons why a plan will not work. The spiritual side of Philip was quick to respond to Jesus' call. But his human side was hesitant and pessimistic. Though a man of faith, he often exhibited a weak faith.

We examined this story when we studied the character of Andrew, but now we will look at it through Philip's eyes. The scene begins with Jesus traveling across the Sea of Galilee. A great multitude followed Him, "because they saw His signs which He performed on those who were diseased" (John 6:2). Jesus went with His disciples up a mountain, where He saw the throng of people coming toward them (see verses 3–5a). In this moment, late in the day, Jesus asked Philip, "Where shall we buy bread, that these may eat?" (verse 5b).

The other disciples likely assumed that Jesus aimed His question at Philip because he was the apostolic administrator—the bean counter responsible for coordinating meals, handling logistics, and organizing resources. We know that Judas was in charge of keeping the money (see 13:29), so it makes sense that someone else was charged with coordinating the acquisition and distribution of meals and supplies. It was a task that suited Philip's personality. However, as John reveals, this was not the reason why Jesus posed the question to him. Rather, Jesus said this "to test him, for He Himself knew what He would do" (John 6:6).

When posed with this dilemma, Philip no doubt started counting heads and crunching numbers. But it was no use. Including the women and children, the crowd was easily ten thousand people or more, and the disciples collectively had only about eight months' worth of funds saved up. This was barely enough to cover their basic operating expenses and nowhere near enough to give so much as a bite of food to everyone in the crowd.

Philip put the impossibility to Jesus straight: "Two hundred denarii worth of bread is not sufficient for them, that every one of them may have a little" (verse 7). From a material perspective, he was right—the disciples could never feed the crowd. But this wasn't a test of logistical thinking. It was a spiritual test needing spiritual eyes. Philip had been present when Jesus turned water to wine (see John 2:2). He had witnessed many miracles of Jesus, including several creative and re-generative miracles. Yet when he saw the crowd, he began to feel overwhelmed by the impossible and lapsed into his old materialistic thinking.

THE FEEDING OF THE FIVE THOUSAND

The feeding of the five thousand is the only miracle recorded in all four Gospels (see Matthew 14:13–23; Mark 6:30–46; Luke 9:10–17; John 6:1–14). John's account of the miracle emphasized its importance in two ways: (1) it demonstrated the creative power of Jesus more clearly than any other miracle, and (2) it supported John's purposes of demonstrating the deity of Jesus while also serving to set the stage for Jesus' discourse on the "bread of life" (see 6:22–40). Interestingly, both creative miracles of Jesus—the turning of water into wine (see 2:1–10) and the multiplying of bread—speak of the elements in the Lord's Supper (see 6:53).[2]

One of the must-haves of a godly leader is *vision*—and this is especially true for followers of Christ. Philip was blinded by unbelief. He allowed arithmetic, human reasoning, and raw data to get in the way and obscure his view of the Lord's limitless capabilities. In all his calculations, he had failed to factor in the difference that Jesus can make.

Jesus taught His disciples, "If you have faith as a mustard seed, you will say to this mountain, 'Move from here to there,' and it will move; and nothing will be impossible for you" (Matthew 17:20). Philip needed to learn this lesson. As long as he limited himself to his own understanding and his own solutions, *everything* would seem impossible to him.

- Read John 2:1–11. How did the situation at the wedding in Cana resemble the situation on the mountainside? Philip had witnessed this miracle, so why do you think he was still having trouble looking past the "numbers" and believing in God's provision?

  _____
  _____
  _____
  _____
  _____
  _____
  _____

- Reread John 6:5–7. Given what Philip had seen Jesus do in previously impossible situations, what should Philip have said? What would have been a better response for him to make?

  _____
  _____
  _____
  _____
  _____
  _____
  _____

● Read Matthew 21:21–22. What does Jesus remind His disciples here about faith? What are some rewards of faith that Philip shut down by failing to consider Jesus' power?

_____

_____

_____

_____

_____

● In what ways are you like Philip when it comes to being hesitant and pessimistic? How would you like God to increase your faith in Him today?

_____

_____

_____

_____

_____

Uncertain and Indecisive

The story of the Greeks in Jerusalem who wished to see Jesus provides us with further insights into Philip's temperament. Once again, we examined this story when we discussed the character of Andrew, but now we will look at it from Philip's perspective. In this instance, we find a man so analytical that he lacked certainty. When he was given another opportunity to walk by faith, he got caught up in protocol and handed over the decision to someone else.

As you might recall, this story takes place after Jesus' triumphal entry into Jerusalem during the week leading up to his arrest and crucifixion. The Greeks were either God-fearing Gentiles or proselytes to Judaism who had come to Jerusalem to worship God at the Passover. Naturally, they were interested in meeting Jesus. Perhaps they sought out Philip to make the connection because of his Greek name. Or maybe they had learned that he was more or less the one who made all the arrangements on behalf of the disciples.

Whatever the reason, these individuals presumed that Philip was Jesus' meeting organizer. It was a simple and straightforward request, yet, for some reason, Philip appears uncertain and indecisive (see John 12:20–21). Being a by-the-book kind of guy, it is possible he was recalling Jesus' previous instructions to "not go into the way of the Gentiles [nor] enter a city of the Samaritans" (Matthew 10:5). Or maybe he was recalling the time when Jesus said, "I was not sent except to the lost sheep of the house of Israel" (15:24).

Only an overanalytical rule-follower like Philip would question whether this meant that Gentiles should not be introduced to Jesus. Had Philip considered the big picture, he might have remembered the time when Jesus offered to come to the home of a centurion to heal his servant (see Matthew 8:5–7). Or when He went out of His way to meet a Samaritan woman (see John 4:1–26). Or when He taught and healed those in a Gentile region for *three days* (see Matthew 15:29–32). Jesus' ministry *priority* was to the Jew first (see Romans 2:10), which meant His words about the Gentiles were a general principle rather than an edict set in stone.

Thankfully, Philip had the heart, and the good sense, to introduce the Greeks to Andrew, whom he knew would bring anyone to Jesus (see John 12:22). In this, we can give Philip credit. Even if he was unsure about introducing them to Jesus himself, he seemed to understand at the least that turning them away completely was not the answer. Philip seemed to know that in his heart, even if his head was obsessed with protocol and procedure.

JESUS' RECEPTION OF THE GREEKS

We can safely assume that Jesus received the Greeks gladly. After all, He Himself had said, "The one who comes to Me I will by no means cast out" (John 6:37). John doesn't record anything about Jesus' meeting with the Greeks except the discourse that Jesus gave on that occasion, in which He said, "If anyone serves Me, let him follow Me; and where I am, there My servant will be also. If anyone serves Me, him My Father will honor" (12:26). In short, Jesus preached the gospel to the Greeks and invited them to become His disciples.[3]

So, what became of Philip? Tradition tells us that he was greatly used in the spread of the early church. By most accounts, he was put to death as a result of his faith by stoning at Heliopolis, in Phrygia (Asia Minor), eight years after the martyrdom of James. Before his death, multitudes came to Christ under his preaching. Philip overcame the human tendencies that often hampered his faith, reminding us in the process that God can use *anyone* for His glory.

- Read John 6:37–40. What was Jesus' promise to all who come to Him? Based on this, what we can assume was Jesus' response in meeting with the Greeks?

  _____

  _____

  _____

  _____

  _____

- Read Matthew 23:13. Jesus issued these strong words against the Jewish scribes and Pharisees. What was the nature of Jesus' complaint against them?

  _____

  _____

  _____

  _____

  _____

- Read James 2:1–4. What does James say in this passage about showing partiality? What does this passage say about who is welcome in God's family?

  _____

  _____

  _____

  _____

- In what ways are you like Philip when it comes to being uncertain and in-decisive? What are some of the ways that God has given you discernment?

_____

_____

_____

_____

_____

CONSIDERING YOUR STORY

Read John 14:7–11. Philip wasn't the only disciple who struggled to grasp the truths that Jesus taught. Yet his earthbound thinking seemed to consistently narrow his spiritual vision.

- Jesus had just made a claim about His divinity—that He and the Father are of the same essence. The disciples had seen Jesus and knew Him, so in effect, they knew the Father as well. What does Philip's question reveal about his lack of understanding this truth?

_____

_____

_____

_____

_____

- When is a time you sought more proof of Christ's divine power, divinity, or grace? When did you realize that what He has provided is already sufficient?

_____

_____

_____

_____

- Philip was slow to understand, slow to trust, and slow to see beyond the moment. Yet church history says he was instrumental in establishing the early church and, prior to his martyrdom, countless people came to Jesus through his preaching. With his story in view, how do you want the Lord to likewise help you in each of these situations?

Quicker to understand:

Quicker to trust:

Quicker to see beyond the moment:

APPLYING TO YOUR LIFE

We can all be thankful that the Lord doesn't disqualify the bean counters. As you reflect on the tendencies that hamper your spiritual vision the most, where could you use a greater, broader, or higher vision? How is the Holy Spirit drawing you to seek Christ above all?

_____

_____

_____

_____

_____

_____

_____

_____

_____

_____

_____

_____

_____

_____

_____

CLOSING PRAYER

Heavenly Father, I have gotten in Your way more times than I can count. But I am willing to learn a new response. So, every time I am staring at difficulties that are far beyond me, please turn my thoughts toward You instead. Bring Your greatness, Your promises, and Your miracles to mind so I don't get lost in the limitations of the moment. Help me recognize that You are always there and always willing to provide. Thank You for spiritual eyes to see. Amen.

Notes

1. John MacArthur, author and general editor, *The MacArthur Study Bible* (Nashville, TN: Thomas Nelson, 1997), notes on Acts 6:1, 5; 8:5.

2. MacArthur, *The MacArthur Study Bible*, note on John 6:1–14.

3. John MacArthur, *Twelve Ordinary Men* (Nashville, TN: Thomas Nelson, 2002), 129–130.

LESSON 7

NATHANAEL

THE GUILELESS ONE

Nathanael said to [Philip],
"Can anything good come out of Nazareth?"

JOHN 1:46

Nathanael is listed as Bartholomew in all four lists of the twelve disciples. He is always called Nathanael in the Gospel of John. Bartholomew is a Hebrew surname meaning "son of Tolmai." So, this disciple of Jesus is Nathanael, the son of Tolmai, or Nathanael Bar-Tolmai. He came from Cana in Galilee, the place where Jesus performed His first miracle (see John 2:1–12).

Nathanael goes unmentioned in the Gospels and the book of Acts except for the lists of the disciples and two passages in the Gospel of John. John portrays Nathanael's calling in his opening chapter (see 1:43–51) and then names him in a scene in his final chapter (see 21:1–3), when the resurrected Jesus appears to seven of His disciples before His ascension.

Nathanael and Philip, who plays an important role in his calling, are another pair within the group of disciples who are always cited together biblically. Although these two were not biological brothers like Peter and Andrew or James and John, the sons of Zebedee, it appears that Philip and Nathanael were as close as brothers. Their brotherhood in the faith is certainly evident from the first recorded interaction between them.

As we discussed in the previous lesson, Jesus had said to Philip, "Follow Me" (John 1:43), and Philip had readily accepted His invitation. Philip's next thought was to find his friend Nathanael, for he knew that he would be interested in learning the long-awaited Messiah they had been seeking had been identified. Nathanael, like Philip, also didn't let the opportunity pass him by. Although he expressed skepticism when he learned the Messiah hailed from Nazareth, his personal interaction with Jesus confirmed that He was the Son of God.

Nathanael, the sixth disciple whom Jesus called to follow Him, came to full understanding and total commitment on day one. He evidently ended just as well as he began. Each church tradition states that he ultimately brought the gospel to Persia, Armenia, and even as far away as India. There is no reliable record of how he died—one report says he was drowned at sea while another states he was crucified—but by all accounts, he died a martyr's death just like all of the other disciples of Jesus (with the exception of John).

A Close Friendship

In the earliest church histories and many of the early legends about the apostles, the names of Philip and Nathanael are often linked. Apparently, they were friends throughout the years of their journey with Christ. Not unlike Peter and Andrew (who were so often named together as brothers) and James and John (who likewise were brothers), we find these two always side by side, not as brothers, but as close companions. Whether this was a business relationship, a family relationship, or just a social relationship, Scripture does not say. But Philip obviously was close to Nathanael and knew that his friend would want to meet Jesus.[1]

We *do* know that Nathanael was a faithful follower of Jesus from the start of his time with Jesus to his final days on this earth. All that he experienced during his time with Jesus, and in his years of ministry, served to root his faith and commitment more firmly. Nathanael stands as proof that God can take ordinary people, from ordinary places, and use them for His glory.

STARTING OUT

How would you describe your level of commitment when it comes to sticking with a task? Are you able to persevere until the job is done or do you tend to burn out and get frustrated?

_____

_____

_____

_____

_____

_____

_____

_____

EXPLORING THE STORY

Even though there is only one narrative about Nathanael from the Gospel of John, there is a lot we can glean about this disciple's character from that story. In particular, we find that Nathanael had a *love of Scripture*, possessed a *sincerity of heart*, and demonstrated an *eager faith*—even though, it must also be said, he was inclined to hold a *prejudice against others*. You will explore each of these aspects of Nathanael's nature in this section.

Love of Scripture

In the previous lesson, we touched on the fact that Philip had been eagerly awaiting the coming of the Messiah. The way that Philip announced his discovery to

Nathanael that Jesus *was* this Messiah is telling: "We have found Him of whom Moses in the law, and also the prophets, wrote" (John 1:45). Clearly, Philip knew the truth of Scripture was something that mattered to Nathanael, so he told him about the Messiah from the standpoint of Old Testament prophecy.

This seems to indicate that Nathanael was Philip's "study partner" when it came to the Scriptures. In all likelihood, they had spent time together going over the books of the Law and the Prophets to learn all they could about the Messiah—and had come to the wilderness together to hear John the Baptist preach. This time and effort would lead Nathanael to immediately discern and acknowledge that Jesus was the "Son of God" (verse 49).

There is one other interesting aspect of Philip's announcement to Nathanael. Notice he said the Messiah was "Jesus of Nazareth, the son of Joseph" (verse 45). Why this clarification? "Jesus" (or *Y'shua* in its Aramaic form) was actually a common name—the same name rendered "Joshua" in the Old Testament. So Philip clarified *this* Jesus was from Nazareth and was the "son of Joseph," using the phrase as a kind of surname ("Jesus Bar-Joseph," just as his friend was "Nathanael Bar-Tolmai"). This was how people were commonly identified in that day.

- Read Psalm 1:1–3. Nathanael had a love of Scripture. What are some of the benefits listed for the person who likewise loves and follows God's Word?

  _____

  _____

  _____

  _____

  _____

- Read Psalm 119:97–106. How would you describe the psalmist's attitude toward Scripture? What does it mean that God's Word is a "lamp" for our feet?

  _____

  _____

  _____

  _____

  _____

- Read 2 Timothy 3:14–17. What did Paul compel Timothy to keep doing? What are some of the ways that Paul states the Bible is "useful" in our lives?

  _____

  _____

  _____

  _____

- How would you describe *your* attitude toward God's Word? What would it take for you to develop the same heart for Scripture that Nathanael had?

  _____

  _____

  _____

  _____

Prejudice Against Others

Nathanael's response to Philip's comment about Jesus' place of origin is telling: "Can anything good come out of Nazareth?" (John 1:46). This is not a well-reasoned response that you would expect of a longtime student of the Bible. Rather, it reveals Nathanael's prejudices.

SCORN FOR NAZARETH

While Galileans were despised by Judeans, Galileans themselves despised those who were from Nazareth. In light of the Pharisees' comment about Jesus in John 7:52—that "no prophet has arisen out of Galilee"—Nathanael's scorn may have centered in the fact that Nazareth was an insignificant village without seeming prophetic importance (see, however, Matthew 2:23). Later, some would contemptuously refer to Christians as "the sect of the Nazarenes" (Acts 24:5).[2]

What is ironic about Nathanael's statement is that his hometown was *Cana*, a small village located in the hills to the north of Nazareth. In Nathanael's day, just as in our day, the village was unprestigious and unexceptional. Nazareth, at least, was on a crossroads, and people passed through it to reach Galilee from the Mediterranean. No one passed through the village of Cana if they didn't have to do so. It was that far off the beaten path.

No doubt, this indicates that much of Nathanael's contempt toward Nazareth was a matter of regional rivalry, much like how someone from Pittsburgh might make snide remarks about someone from Cleveland. Nathanael's comment also reflects the general attitude toward the Nazarenes at that time. For Nathanael, the fact that the Messiah would come out of low-class *Nazareth* was almost unfathomable.

Nathanael's attitude in this regard reflects the opinion of most of the people of Israel. They were also not expecting the Messiah to come out of a town like Nazareth. After all, it was an uncultured place populated by evil, corrupt, and sinful people. Surely, they reasoned, the Messiah would be identified with Jerusalem, for He was to reign in Jerusalem. This prejudice blocked their view of the Messiah and their receptivity to the gospel. In their minds, Jesus was from the wrong place. He wasn't trained within the official religious establishment. His message was an offense. So they rejected Him—and then tried to silence Him permanently.

This happens even today. We are all guilty at times of holding prejudicial beliefs about individuals, classes of people, or even entire societies. Fortunately, Nathanael's prejudice wasn't strong enough to keep him from Christ. When Philip beckoned his friend Nathanael to "come and see" *this* particular Nazarene (John 1:46), Nathanael agreed and went.

● Read John 7:37–44. Nathanael was not the only person who expressed skepticism about the Messiah coming out of Galilee. What does this passage reveal about the different reactions to Jesus? What does it reveal about the Israelites' expectations of the Messiah?

_____

_____

_____

_____

- Read Mark 6:1–6. How did the people of Jesus' hometown react to His teaching in the synagogue? Why were they unable to view Him as the Messiah?

  _____

  _____

  _____

  _____

- Read 2 Corinthians 4:3–4. What metaphors does the apostle Paul use to describe people's prejudice? Why are people often "blind" when it comes to seeing what God is doing in their midst?

  _____

  _____

  _____

  _____

- What are some prejudicial beliefs you might be holding against others? What does Nathanael's story reveal about the dangers of holding such prejudices?

  _____

  _____

  _____

  _____

Sincerity of Heart

Jesus Himself speaks to the most important aspect of Nathanael's character: _his sincerity of heart._ When He saw Nathanael coming toward Him, He declared that he was a man "in whom is no deceit" (John 1:47). This was an incredible compliment!

It is one thing to hear, "Well done, good and faithful servant" (Matthew 25:21) at the end of one's life. But to be commended by Jesus from the _start_ speaks volumes about the state of Nathanael's heart. Jesus' words "an Israelite indeed" (which in the Hebrew means "truly, genuinely," rather than "physically descended from Abraham") only reinforce the affirmation.

Of course, Nathanael was prone to sin, just like the rest of us. What Jesus was seeing was that his heart had not been darkened by *hypocrisy* like so many others in first-century Israel. The Jewish religious leaders wore a veneer of spirituality (see Jesus' indictment of them in Matthew 23:13–33) and were always trying to "catch Him in His words" (Mark 12:13). Nathanael, however, was a genuine worshiper of God with no hypocrisy. His spiritual devotion was real. He was a righteous man with a sincere heart devoted to God.

- Read Romans 2:25–29. Jesus described Nathanael in John 1:47 as "an Israelite indeed." What does Paul say is the difference in being a Jew (a follower of God's law) inwardly rather than outwardly? What does he mean when he refers to circumcision of the heart?

  _____

  _____

  _____

  _____

  _____

  _____

- Read Matthew 6:1–4. Jesus often had strong words for those who made a show of their faith on the outside to receive the praise of others. What is Jesus' caution in this passage when it comes to doing good works? What "reward" should His followers seek?

  _____

  _____

  _____

  _____

  _____

● Read James 4:8–10. What instructions does James provide in this passage for those who want to genuinely and sincerely worship God with no hypocrisy in their hearts?

_____

_____

_____

_____

● What stands out about Nathanael when it comes to the sincerity of his heart? In what ways is God helping you to develop a sincere heart that is completely devoted to Him?

_____

_____

_____

_____

Eager Faith

Jesus' comments about Nathanael being "an Israelite indeed" whose heart contained "no deceit" prompted him to declare, "How do You know me?" (John 1:47–48). Nathanael might have been wondering if Jesus was just trying to flatter him. Nazareth did not fit into any of the prophecies about the Messiah. In fact, the town did not even *exist* in Old Testament times. Furthermore, Jesus was the son of a local carpenter. Was He just paying compliments to Nathanael in an attempt to compel him to become one of His disciples?

Jesus assured Nathanael of His authenticity with His next statement: "Before Philip called you, when you were under the fig tree, I saw you" (verse 48). Nathanael would have seen in this that Jesus wasn't *flattering* him but actually knew *about* him. Jesus had not been physically present to see Nathanael under the fig tree—which was most likely the place he went to study Scripture and pray. In effect, Jesus was affirming him again, saying, "I know what you were doing there. I saw you in that place seeking after Me."

"UNDER THE FIG TREE, I SAW YOU"

Not only was Jesus' brief summary of Nathanael accurate (see John 1:47), but the Lord also revealed information that could only be known by Nathanael himself. Perhaps Nathanael had some significant or outstanding experience of communion with God at the location, and he was able to recognize Jesus' allusion to it. At any rate, Jesus had knowledge of this event not available to men.[3]

The only explanation as to how Jesus could know this was *omniscience*. Nathanael recognized this truth at that moment and answered, "Rabbi, You are the Son of God! You are the King of Israel!" (verse 49). Nathanael's knowledge of the Old Testament had clearly impressed on him that the Messiah would be both the Son of God (see Psalm 2) and the King of Israel (see Zephaniah 3:15; Zechariah 9:9; Micah 5:2). Ironically, it was this same truth that would escape his friend Philip after they had spent nearly three years with Jesus (see John 14:8-9). What Philip didn't get until the end, Nathanael understood at the very beginning.

No one could ever call Nathanael one of the half-hearted. He came to full understanding and total commitment on day one. Jesus recognized Nathanael's faith and said, "Because I said to you, 'I saw you under the fig tree,' do you believe? You will see greater things than these" (John 1:50). Jesus promised that Nathanael would see much more than just this simple display of His omniscience. He would witness things that would serve to enrich and enlarge his faith.

● Read Isaiah 55:8-9. How does God do things in our world? What should we believe when we see God moving in ways we don't expect?

_____

_____

_____

_____

_____

- Read Psalm 139:1–6. Nathanael was amazed at Jesus' omniscience in seeing him beneath the fig tree. What does this passage say about all that God knows about us?

  _____

  _____

  _____

  _____

  _____

  _____

- Read John 20:30–31. What was John's intent in writing his Gospel? Why is a testimony like Nathanael's—that Jesus is the Son of God—so important for us to grasp today?

  _____

  _____

  _____

  _____

  _____

  _____

- What stands out to you about Nathanael when it comes to his faith in Christ? What are some of the ways that God has built your trust and faith in Him over the course of your life?

  _____

  _____

  _____

  _____

  _____

  _____

CONSIDERING YOUR STORY

Read Luke 24:13–27. Most of the disciples struggled long and hard to get to where Nathanael was after his *first* meeting with Jesus. For Nathanael, what Jesus did after he became a disciple didn't prove that Jesus was the Messiah but rather affirmed what he already knew to be true.

● What were the two men discussing as they made their way to Emmaus? How did Jesus help them understand that everything that had happened was according to the Scriptures?

_____

_____

_____

_____

_____

● What are some of the benefits you have received from studying God's Word?

_____

_____

_____

_____

_____

● As you reflect on Nathanael's character, circle the qualities below that you also have or would like to have. Underline the qualities that you most want to be present in your life.

Love of Scripture	Discernment	Confidence
Sincerity of heart	Honesty	Faith in God
Trust in God	Commitment to Christ	Faithfulness

APPLYING TO YOUR LIFE

As followers of Jesus, we are to "run with endurance the race that is set before us, looking unto Jesus, the author and finisher of our faith" (Hebrews 12:1–2). How are you running the "race" when it comes to your faith in Christ? How are you keeping your focus on Jesus as you run?

_____

_____

_____

_____

_____

_____

_____

_____

_____

_____

_____

_____

_____

_____

_____

_____

_____

CLOSING PRAYER

Jesus, You have said that the pure in heart are blessed and will see You. Please draw me more and more to Your Word and into spending time with You. As You do, I ask You to purify my faith and open my eyes to see all of who You are. Thank You for the confidence Your faithfulness provides. Having You as my God and my King who has, and will, fulfill every biblical prophecy gives me hope for today and for tomorrow. I bless Your holy name. Amen.

Notes

1. John MacArthur, *Twelve Ordinary Men* (Nashville, TN: Thomas Nelson, 2002), 136.
2. John MacArthur, author and general editor, *The MacArthur Study Bible* (Nashville, TN: Thomas Nelson, 1997), note on John 1:46.
3. MacArthur, *The MacArthur Study Bible*, note on John 1:48.

MATTHEW AND THOMAS

THE TAX COLLECTOR AND THE TWIN

As Jesus passed on from there, He saw a man named Matthew sitting at the tax office. And He said to him, "Follow Me." So he arose and followed Him.

MATTHEW 9:9

Then Thomas, who is called the Twin, said to his fellow disciples, "Let us also go, that we may die with Him."

JOHN 11:16

The prophet Isaiah said of the Lord, "He brings down those who dwell on high, the lofty city; He lays it low, He lays it low to the ground, He brings it down to the dust. The foot shall tread it down—the feet of the poor and the steps of the needy" (Isaiah 26:5-6). Given this, it is little wonder that we find Jesus shunning the "lofty" religious elites in choosing His disciples and instead seeking out the ordinary. This is, after all, how it has always been in God's economy. He exalts the humble and lays low the proud (see Ezekiel 21:26; Matthew 23:12; James 4:6).

Jesus' complaint against the religious leaders of Israel—like the scribes and the Pharisees—was that they were acting as "blind guides" (Matthew 23:16). In truth, most members of the Jewish establishment were so spiritually blind that even when Jesus did miracles before their eyes, they could not see Him as the Messiah. They saw Him instead as a threat and an enemy and "plotted against Him, how they might destroy Him" (12:14).

It wasn't that the religious leaders doubted Jesus performed miracles. After all, who *could* deny the results? There were too many miracles, and they had been done too publicly to be discounted. While some tried to claim that Jesus performed His miracles by the power of Satan (see 12:24), no one actually denied the miracles were real. What actually made the religious elite infuriated at Jesus was not the miracles but the fact that He called them sinners. When Jesus, like John the Baptist before Him, preached a message of repentance and said *they* were sinners in need of God's forgiveness, that crossed a line in their minds.

It was thus because of Jesus' message that they vilified Him, rejected Him, and ultimately executed Him. This is precisely why, when it came time for Jesus to select His disciples, He chose lowly and common men. He needed followers who were willing to acknowledge their own sinfulness and who were unafraid to have their spiritual eyes opened. Ordinary men like Matthew and Thomas.

STARTING OUT

What are some examples of spiritual blindness in our world today? What are some of the ways you have seen God open people's eyes to the truth of the gospel?

_____

_____

_____

_____

_____

_____

_____

_____

EXPLORING THE STORY

In all likelihood, none of the twelve disciples was more notorious of a sinner than Matthew. So it is surprising to read how Jesus gave him *a new calling* and how this led to Matthew gaining *a new perspective* on his sinful state. We also read how another disciple named Thomas demonstrated *a courageous heart* in agreeing to accompany Jesus to Bethany and how, after the resurrection, his spiritual eyes were opened and he received *renewed hope*. You will explore stories from the Gospels related to these two disciples in the following section.

Matthew's New Calling

Matthew is a Greek name that likely derives from the Hebrew name Mattaniah (see 1 Chronicles 9:15), which means "gift of God." Matthew's Jewish name was Levi, and Mark and Luke use this name in their story about his calling (see Mark 2:13–17; Luke 5:27–32). However, Luke refers to him as Matthew in his lists of the twelve disciples (see Luke 6:16; Acts 1:13). Mark adds the detail that he was "Levi the son of Alphaeus" (Mark 2:14), which is the same name as another disciple's father (see Matthew 10:3), though it is unlikely they were brothers.

What sets Matthew apart from the rest of the disciples is his occupation. Matthew was a tax collector (or publican), which meant that he was among the most despised people in society—sometimes grouped with prostitutes in terms of social standing (see Matthew 21:32). The job of tax collectors was to collect

TAX COLLECTORS

Tax collectors were despised in Israel. They were hated and vilified by all of Jewish society. They were deemed lower than Herodians (Jews loyal to the Idumean dynasty of Herods) and more worthy of scorn than the occupying Roman soldiers. Publicans were men who had bought tax franchises from the Roman emperor and then extorted money from the people of Israel to feed the Roman coffers and to pad their own pockets. They often strong-armed money out of people with the use of thugs. Most were despicable, vile, unprincipled scoundrels.[1]

a certain amount of funds for the Roman government, but they often extorted extra amounts to fill their own personal coffers.

Matthew was even more reviled because he was a Jew. If tax collectors entered a home, all that was in it was considered unclean, and they were forbidden from entering the synagogues. Jewish tax collectors were thus essentially cut off from their community and places of worship. Given this, Matthew must have been shocked when Jesus chose him. Luke reports his reaction was immediate: "He left all, rose up, and followed Him" (5:28).

The scene as Matthew describes it in his own Gospel is surprisingly undramatic. Jesus saw him sitting at the tax office, said, "Follow Me," and Matthew instantly and without hesitation "arose and followed Him" (9:9). There was no shortage of money-grubbers waiting in the wings to get their chance at his business. Once Matthew walked away, he knew that he could never go back. Yet he never regretted his decision to answer Jesus' call.

- Read Matthew 9:9–13 and Mark 1:16–20. What are similarities between Jesus' calling of Matthew and His calling of the fishermen? What similarities are there between Matthew's response to Jesus' call and the fishermen's?

  _____
  _____
  _____
  _____
  _____
  _____

- Read Luke 18:18–23. What invitation did Jesus extend to the man? What difference do you see in the way he responded as compared to Matthew, Andrew, Peter, James, and John?

  _____
  _____
  _____
  _____
  _____

- Read Luke 5:27–32. Based on Matthew's actions, what do you gather about his state of mind (and heart) at the time that Jesus came along? What did Jesus mean when He said that He had come to minister to people just like Matthew and his friends?

  _____

  _____

  _____

  _____

  _____

- What encouragement do you gain from Matthew's story about the kinds of people whom God calls to serve in His kingdom?

  _____

  _____

  _____

  _____

Matthew's New Perspective

Matthew moves from his brief narrative about his calling to a dinner party attended by Jesus, His disciples, and "many tax collectors and sinners" (9:10). Luke reveals that this was actually a "great feast in [Matthew's] own house" (5:29) to honor Jesus. Yet this was no elitist event. It was just Matthew's friends—people who were deemed to be social outcasts.

As we saw in previous lessons, Andrew's and Philip's first impulse after answering Jesus' call was to find their closest friends and introduce them to the Savior. Matthew did exactly the same. He was so thrilled to have found the Messiah that he wanted to introduce Jesus to everyone he knew. So he held a large banquet in Jesus' honor and invited them all.

Of course, this did not escape the notice of the scribes and the Pharisees. They were outraged that Jesus would celebrate anything with these kinds of people. So they approached His disciples and said, "How is it that He eats and drinks with tax collectors and sinners?" (Mark 2:16). Jesus replied, "Those who are well

THE PHARISEES' COMPLAINT

Matthew's response to Jesus' call was to invite the Lord to a dinner party in his home where he could introduce his former comrades to Christ. For the Pharisees, this was outrageous. In their minds, consorting with outcasts on any level—merely speaking to them—was bad enough. But eating and drinking with them implied a level of friendship that was absolutely abhorrent (see Luke 7:34; 15:2; 19:7).[2]

have no need of a physician, but those who are sick. I did not come to call the righteous, but sinners, to repentance" (verse 17).

Matthew recognized his need. As a tax collector, he knew his greed, sin, and betrayal of his own people. Even though he had been excluded from the synagogues, he knew the Old Testament well. (In fact, he quotes from it more than the three other Gospel writers combined.) He had surely also heard the fantastic stories about Jesus as he sat in his tax booth day after day. Matthew's tortured soul had finally yielded to the truth about himself: Deep down inside, he was a Jew with an undeniable spiritual hunger.

All these things produced a divine readiness that prepared him to drop everything without a second thought—including a lucrative career—and devote himself to Jesus. Forever grateful for forgiveness and a fresh start, Matthew humbly embraced the outcasts and ministered to the Jews in Israel and abroad for years until, according to early tradition, he was martyred for his faith. In every way, he gave his all for Christ.

● Read Luke 19:1–10. Zacchaeus was also a despised tax collector. What parallels do you see between his story and the story of Matthew's calling? What new perspective did Zacchaeus gain after his encounter with Jesus?

_____

_____

_____

_____

- Read Luke 18:10–14. This parable from Jesus might recount a real-life incident. What did the tax collector recognize about his condition? How did Jesus use this story to contrast his humble attitude with the prideful attitude of the Jewish religious leaders?

  _____

  _____

  _____

  _____

- Read Luke 15:1–7. What was the complaint of the scribes and Pharisees? How did Jesus respond to their complaint through the parable that He told?

  _____

  _____

  _____

  _____

- What does Matthew's story reveal about the importance of being honest about your sinful condition? What blessing will you receive when you approach God with a repentant heart?

  _____

  _____

  _____

  _____

Thomas's Courageous Heart

While the final disciple in the second group is typically nicknamed "Doubting Thomas," this isn't the most accurate label for the one also known as Didymus (which means "the twin"). He was a better man, with a better heart, than most give him credit for being. However, he could at times be an "Eeyore." He was a worrier and brooder who was always anticipating the storm cloud to come. Pessimism seems to have been more of a struggle for him than doubt. Still, commendable aspects of his character shine through in the one story told about him.

John reports that Jesus had just departed Jerusalem due to threats against his life by the Jewish religious authorities. He traveled with His disciples into the wilderness, where He could minister unhindered (see John 10:39–42). While he was there, a message arrived from Mary and Martha, the sisters of his close friend Lazarus, that he was ill. The sisters, knowing how much Jesus loved their family, anticipated He would hurry back to heal their brother.

Meanwhile, the disciples were concerned because Mary, Martha, and Lazarus lived in Bethany, a town located on the outskirts of Jerusalem. If Jesus went there, His enemies were sure to find out, and that would put both His life and the lives of the disciples in jeopardy (see 11:1–3). So we can imagine their relief when Jesus said, "This sickness is not unto death, but for the glory of God, that the Son of God may be glorified through it" (verse 4). *Tragedy averted*, they mistakenly thought. *Jesus is staying put since Lazarus isn't going to die.*

What the disciples didn't understand was that Lazarus *was* going to die and that Jesus *did* plan to go to Bethany. He just wasn't returning there right away. He waited where He was a few extra days so that Lazarus was already dead for four days before He arrived. He then announced His intent to the disciples to return to Judea (see verses 5–7).

The disciples, understandably, thought this was bad idea. They collectively said to Jesus, "Rabbi, lately the Jews sought to stone You, and are You going there again?" (verse 8). Remember, they thought that Lazarus was on the road to recovery. So Jesus told them plainly, "Lazarus is dead. And I am glad for your sakes that I was not there, that you may believe. Nevertheless let us go to him" (verses 14–15).

This is when Thomas spoke up: "Thomas, who is called the Twin, said to his fellow disciples, 'Let us also go, that we may die with Him'" (verse 16). Here is what we often miss about Thomas. He was indeed expecting catastrophe if they returned to Bethany. Yet, in his firm devotion to Christ, he was still courageously willing to go there. He was resolved to die with Jesus rather than forsake Him. For him, to live without his Lord was inconceivable.

Thomas's bravery evidently strengthened the other disciples, for they all decided to return to Bethany, where Jesus raised Lazarus from the dead. What the disciples feared did not occur at this time, for it was not in God's timing yet for

Jesus to die. However, the Pharisees learned of Jesus' actions and began to plot how to put Him to death (see verses 17–53).

- Read John 11:5–11. The disciples were rightly concerned that returning to Bethany would put Jesus' life in danger. However, Jesus was not willing to skulk around like a criminal—He would do His work in the bright light of the day. Why did Jesus feel such freedom to return to Jerusalem? Who did He say is the one who is actually in danger of stumbling?

  _____
  _____
  _____
  _____
  _____
  _____

- Read John 11:12–16. How might an optimist have responded to Jesus' announcement that He was going to journey to Bethany—especially after hearing His preceding illustration?

  _____
  _____
  _____
  _____
  _____
  _____

- Read John 14:1–7. Jesus knew what the disciples would soon face. So why did He say that the disciples' hearts need not be "troubled"?

  _____
  _____
  _____
  _____
  _____

● Thomas had a courageous heart in spite of his pessimistic outlook. What are some of the ways that God had called you to be courageous for Him?

_____

_____

_____

_____

_____

_____

_____

Thomas's Renewed Hope

We get one further picture of Thomas in a story told at the end of John's Gospel. After Jesus' death, the disciples gathered together for support and out of "fear of the Jews" (John 20:19). Everyone was there except Judas (who had hanged himself after betraying Christ) and, for some reason, Thomas (see verse 24). Suddenly, even though the doors and windows were shut, "Jesus came and stood in the midst, and said to them, 'Peace be with you'" (verse 19).

Why wasn't Thomas there? Possibly he was so grief-stricken that he just wanted to be alone. Nonetheless, his friends came looking for him, and when they found him, they said, "We have seen the Lord" (verse 25). But Thomas, ever the pessimist, wasn't going to be convinced so easily. He told them plainly, "Unless I see in His hands the print of the nails, and put my finger into the print of the nails, and put my hand into His side, I will not believe'" (verse 25).

This is why this disciple of Jesus has come to be known as "Doubting Thomas." But we shouldn't be so hard on him. What set Thomas apart from the other disciples was not that his *doubt* was greater but that his *sorrow* was greater. In truth, *all* of the disciples were slow to accept that Jesus had risen. They *all* had to see Jesus in the flesh before they believed.

Eight days later, Jesus appeared to the disciples again, and this time Thomas was with them (see verse 26). Jesus said to Thomas, "Reach your finger here, and look at My hands; and reach your hand here, and put it into My side. Do not be unbelieving, but believing" (verse 27). Jesus understood Thomas's doubt and sympathized with his uncertainty.

THE COMPASSION OF CHRIST

Thomas erred because he was wired to be a pessimist. But it was the error of a profound love. It was provoked by grief, brokenheartedness, uncertainty, and the pain of loneliness. No one could feel the way Thomas felt unless he loved Jesus the way Thomas loved Him. So Jesus was tender with him. He understands our weaknesses (see Hebrews 4:15). So He understands our doubt. He sympathizes with our uncertainty. He is patient with our pessimism. And while recognizing these as weaknesses, we must also acknowledge Thomas's heroic devotion to Christ, which made him understand that it would be better to die than to be separated from his Lord. The proof of his love was the profoundness of his despair.[3]

Thomas's melancholy melted away at the sight of Jesus standing in his midst. He cried out, "My Lord and my God!" (verse 28). In that moment, he was transformed into a great evangelist. Shortly after, he was filled with the Holy Spirit on the Day of Pentecost and empowered for ministry. Ancient accounts state that he took the gospel as far as India and was martyred by being run through with a spear. If this account is true, it is a fitting end for one whose faith came to fruition when he saw the spear mark in his Master's side.

● Read Mark 16:9–13. Based on this passage, what did Thomas have in common with other disciples of Jesus?

_____

_____

_____

_____

_____

_____

_____

_____

- Read John 20:19–20. Jesus came and physically stood in the midst of ten of the disciples after His resurrection. What did He show them at this time?

  _____

  _____

  _____

  _____

  _____

- Read John 20:24–28. Thomas wanted physical proof before he would believe in Jesus' resurrection. How did the Lord meet these specific requests?

  _____

  _____

  _____

  _____

  _____

- Thomas's declaration that Jesus was his Lord and his God reveals that his hope had been renewed. In what ways do you need Christ to likewise renew your hope in Him today?

  _____

  _____

  _____

  _____

  _____

CONSIDERING YOUR STORY

Read Hebrews 4:12–16. The Lord not only sees our sin, as He saw in Matthew, but also discerns what is in our hearts and offers forgiveness. He is patient with our pessimism, as He was with Thomas, and sympathizes with us in our uncertainties.

● How has Jesus' redemption, forgiveness, understanding, and compassion personally strengthened your belief in Him and given you renewed hope?

_____

_____

_____

_____

● Think about a time you've shared with someone else that story of how Jesus strengthened you. What difference did it make in that person's life?

_____

_____

_____

_____

● Early church accounts report that both Matthew and Thomas held fast to their hope in Jesus to the very end of their lives. Look up the following additional passages and write down what they say about the hope that you can also have in Christ.

John 3:16–18:

2 Corinthians 4:16–18:

1 Peter 1:3–6:

APPLYING TO YOUR LIFE

It is remarkable that God not only *could* but *did* use a vile sinner and a melancholy pessimist for His glory. In which area(s) of your life—perhaps your temperament, line of work, or the effects of your past—does He seem to be saying, "I know this is a problem for you, but I am the answer, so acknowledge it and bring it to Me"? Where is He offering you *newness* today?

_____

_____

_____

_____

_____

_____

_____

_____

_____

_____

_____

_____

CLOSING PRAYER

Lord God, I've been holding back and unwilling to let You have Your way because I've been afraid of change, afraid to confess, afraid of others' reactions, and afraid of what following You might cost me. But I want the peace, confidence, and hope that You supply in surrender. Today, I'm choosing to believe in Your thoroughly transforming power. In Your name. Amen.

Notes

1. John MacArthur, *Twelve Ordinary Men* (Nashville, TN: Thomas Nelson, 2002), 151–152.
2. John MacArthur, author and general editor, *The MacArthur Study Bible* (Nashville, TN: Thomas Nelson, 1997), notes on Luke 5:29 and Luke 5:30.
3. MacArthur, *Twelve Ordinary Men*, 164.

JAMES (THE LESS), SIMON (THE ZEALOT), AND JUDAS (NOT ISCARIOT)

THE NOT-SO-WELL-KNOWN TRIO

James the son of Alphaeus, and Simon called the Zealot; Judas the son of James . . .

LUKE 6:15–16

The final group of four disciples is the least known to us, except for Judas Iscariot, who is notorious for betraying Christ. Based on their absence from the Gospel accounts, they seem to have been less intimate with Jesus than the other disciples. Yet we must not forget that they also gave up everything to follow after

Jesus and become His disciples. Peter spoke for each of them when he said, "See, we have left all and followed You" (Luke 18:28).

The disciples we will discuss in this lesson—James (the Less), Simon (the Zealot), and Judas (not Iscariot)—all made heroic sacrifices. Yet we don't get to see that heroicism in the Gospels. In fact, when *any* of the disciples are visible in the biblical story, it is typically to put their weaknesses on display (see Mark 9:14–29). We see them thinking more highly of themselves than they should, or speaking when silence would be wise, or confused about things that Jesus has just said. Time and again, in the amazing honesty of the Gospel accounts, the shortcomings of these ordinary men show up far more than their strengths.

We do see the eleven disciples in a different light after the infilling of the Holy Spirit on the Day of Pentecost. From that point on, we see them making courageous decisions, performing great miracles, and preaching with a newfound boldness. Yet beyond the few stories we find in the book of Acts, we read little else about them in the New Testament. The legacy of the disciples wasn't as biblical celebrities but as the foundation stones of the church (see Ephesians 2:20). The church exists today, more than two thousand years later, because these individuals were willing to take the gospel to the ends of the earth.

The twelve disciples, with the exception of Judas Iscariot, were men of true faith who sacrificed everything to follow Jesus. (Judas's failure to make that commitment, while pretending that he had, was what made him so despicable.) This is the most heroic fact about them—and it stands true not just for the disciples we know well but also for the lesser-known ones such as James the Less, Simon the Zealot, and Judas (not Iscariot).

STARTING OUT

Who is a "silent servant" you know? The one whose name isn't familiar to people yet God has used greatly in your church, or within your family, or even in your own life? What do you appreciate most about the way this person ministers?

EXPLORING THE STORY

As we examine this trio of disciples, we find that even though the Bible has little to say about them, they nonetheless have their own distinctions. In fact, the nicknames they are given can tell us something about them: James *the Less*, Simon *the Zealot*, and Judas *(not Iscariot)*. In this section, you will explore what you can discern about the men given these nicknames.

James the Less

The ninth name in each of the four lists of the disciples is "James the son of Alphaeus" (Matthew 10:3; Mark 3:18; Luke 6:15; Acts 1:13). This is the one thing the Bible tells us about him. If this James ever wrote anything, or if he ever stood before kings or preached to vast crowds, we have no word of it. He is virtually unknown to us. He even had a common name.

The distinction "son of Alphaeus" tells us who this man is *not*. This James is not the son of Zebedee who was in Jesus' close inner circle. Nor was this James another notable person we find in the New Testament—Jesus' half-brother named James, who was a leader in the Jerusalem church (see Acts 15:13–21) and likely the author of the epistle that bears his name.

Besides this James being the son of Alphaeus, we also know that his mother's name was Mary and that she had another son named Joses (see Mark 15:40; Matthew 27:56). Mary was one of few eyewitnesses to Jesus' crucifixion named in the Bible, and she also helped to prepare Christ's body for burial (see Mark 16:1). Joses must have also been a well-known follower of the Lord, as his name is specifically mentioned in two Gospels.

DISAPPEARING ACT

All the disciples more or less disappear from the biblical narrative within a few years after Pentecost. In no case does Scripture give us a full biography. That is because Scripture always keeps the focus on the power of Christ and the power of the Word, not the men who were merely instruments of that power.[1]

Mark reveals that James was nicknamed "the Less" (see Mark 15:40). This could refer to his physical features—perhaps he was short or small-framed. It could also indicate that he was young in age or, at least, younger than the other disciple with the same name. But most likely, it refers to his level of influence. James the son of Zebedee was from a prominent family (see John 18:15–16) *and* part of the Lord's inner circle. We could say that he was "James the Most." Therefore, the son of Alphaeus was known as "James the Less."

It could be that the son of Alphaeus was all these things—a small, young, quiet individual who kept a low profile. Still, he was one of the twelve disciples who was personally selected by Jesus for a reason, trained by Him, filled with the Holy Spirit, and then sent out as a witness just *like the others*. This alone tells us something about the man.

Now, it is possible this James had some pedigree. Based on Mark 2:14, he may have been the brother of Levi (Matthew). Or, comparing Mark 15:40 and John 19:25, he might have been Jesus' cousin. But since Scripture doesn't tell us, the answer isn't important. What made James important was not his lineage but the Lord he served and the message he proclaimed.

There is some evidence that James the Less took the gospel to Syria and Persia. Accounts of his death differ, yet we can be sure that he answered Jesus' call to preach the gospel and performed the "signs and wonders and mighty deeds" of an apostle (2 Corinthians 12:12). Furthermore, even though today we barely know his name, it will be forever etched on one of the foundations of the New Jerusalem (see Revelation 21:14).

- Read John 3:25–30. What did John the Baptist understand about his role? How did he view his "status" and influence as compared to that of Jesus?

  _____

  _____

  _____

  _____

  _____

- Read Hebrews 11:35–38. How do the deeds and spiritual dedication of these unnamed saints "stack up" to the deeds and dedication of the scriptural saints who are familiar to you? What does this say to you about what matters from God's perspective?

_____

_____

_____

_____

_____

- The first words of verse 38 indicate "the world was not worthy" of these people (even the ones whose names we don't know). What does this say about their status in God's eyes?

_____

_____

_____

_____

_____

- What lessons do you learn from James "the Less" about the way God uses even those who prefer to keep a low profile? What inspiration does this provide in your life?

_____

_____

_____

_____

_____

Simon the Zealot

The next name given in Luke's list of the disciples is Simon the Zealot (see Luke 6:15; Acts 1:13). In the lists of apostles in Matthew and Mark, he is called "Simon the Cananite" (Matthew 10:4; Mark 3:18). The designation *Cananite* comes from the Hebrew root word *qanna*, which means "to be zealous." So each designation points to the same meaning.

TWO EXTREMES

As one of the Twelve, Simon had to associate with Matthew, who was at the opposite end of the political spectrum, collecting taxes for the Roman government. At one point in his life, Simon would probably have gladly killed Matthew. In the end, they became spiritual brethren, working side by side for the same cause.[2]

It is possible that Simon had a "zealous" temperament, but more likely he carried the nickname because he was a former member of a political sect known as the Zealots. According to the historian Josephus, the Zealots were one of the four main parties among the Jews of that time (the others being the Pharisees, Sadducees, and Essenes).[2] The Zealots were the most politically minded of the four groups. They believed that only God had the right to rule over the Jews, and so they were hoping for a Messiah who would lead them in overthrowing the Roman government and restore the kingdom to Israel. In the meantime, these extremists sought to advance their agenda through stealth acts of violence.

Josephus described them as being "zealous in the worst actions, and extravagant in them beyond the example of others."[3] What made them even more formidable was that seemingly nothing could extinguish their fanaticism. The Zealots were prepared to suffer any kind of death, torture, or pain for the sake of their cause. Until he met Jesus, Simon was one of these. We don't know what his calling to faith was like, but once he embraced Jesus as his Lord, he turned his now-godly zeal toward introducing new citizens to the eternal kingdom.

Several sources report that Simon took the gospel north to the British Isles. There is no reliable account of how he met his end, but by all accounts he suffered a martyr's death. This former member of an organization that was willing to kill (and be killed) for an earthly political agenda had found a far greater cause—and for that he willingly gave his life.

● Read Matthew 10:4 and Mark 3:18–19. Given the Gospel writers often indicate the pairs among the apostles, who was likely Simon the Zealot's ministry partner? (As a sidenote, they probably both originally followed Jesus for similar political reasons.)

_____

_____

_____

_____

_____

_____

- Read Mark 12:13–17. The Herodians, as the name implies, were a political group who supported the Herodian dynasty in Judea. How did this group (and the Pharisees) try to trap Jesus in "politics"? How did Jesus respond to their question?

_____

_____

_____

_____

_____

_____

- Read Colossians 1:21–23. The disciples came from different backgrounds and contexts that likely conflicted with each other. However, according to Paul, what should every Christian's primary cause be now? What keeps our passions properly directed?

_____

_____

_____

_____

_____

● Have you ever ended up as spiritual kin to somebody who was previously devoted to an opposing cause? If so, what impression has that left on you about God's kingdom?

_____

_____

_____

_____

_____

Judas (not Iscariot)

The last name on the list of faithful disciples is Judas, son of a man named James. The name Judas means "praised," but it was forever marred because of Judas Iscariot. For this reason, when the apostle John mentions him, he specifies "Judas (not Iscariot)" (John 14:22).

Judas the son of James had two other names. He was also called "Lebbaeus, whose surname was Thaddaeus" (Matthew 10:3). These were essentially nicknames. Thaddaeus means "breast child," like a nursing baby. It could derisively refer to a "mama's boy," or maybe he was the youngest of several siblings and therefore the baby of the family. His other name, Lebbaeus, means "heart child." Both names suggest a childlike tenderness.

We don't typically picture a gentle soul like this among the other mostly rough-and-tumble disciples, much less hanging around a group that includes Simon the Zealot. Yet the Lord uses all kinds of personalities and temperaments for His kingdom work. Compassionate and sweet-natured types make great preachers just as much as zealots do.

OBSCURE BUT STILL IMPORTANT

Like the other three faithful members of the third apostolic group, Lebbaeus Thaddaeus is more or less shrouded in obscurity. But that obscurity should not cloud our respect for them. They all became mighty preachers.[5]

John's Gospel provides one quick glimpse of this Judas and his heart for others. During the Last Supper, Jesus said to His disciples, "He who has My commandments and keeps them, it is he who loves Me. And he who loves Me will be loved by My Father, and I will love him and manifest Myself to him" (14:21). This Judas then said to Him, "Lord, how is it that You will manifest Yourself to us, and not to the world?" (verse 22).

Here we see the gentle humility of this man. He was not being brash or overconfident. He was not rebuking the Lord, as if he knew best. His question is full of meekness. He was surprised that Jesus would let this ragtag group of eleven in on the good news of salvation but keep it from everybody else. Given that the gospel is the happiest news for every man, woman, and child, he didn't want anyone to miss out. So Judas Lebbaeus Thaddaeus was innocently asking, "Why are You going to disclose Yourself to us and not to the whole world?"

Jesus' answer was laden with tenderness: "If anyone loves Me, he will keep My word; and My Father will love him, and We will come to him and make Our home with him" (verse 23). In other words, Jesus replied that He would manifest Himself to anyone who loves Him. It was a message that Judas the son of James took into the world. Tradition states he took the gospel to Edessa, a royal city in Mesopotamia, and even brought about the healing of its king.

This tenderhearted servant preached the love and forgiveness of Jesus and then, just like the rest of the better-known disciples, was martyred for his faith. Although his name has been tainted because of the other Judas, his testimony was not. Nothing could stain or hinder the testimony of this disciple who loved the Lord and obeyed His words.

● Read Mark 10:13–16. Judas's nicknames Thaddaeus and Lebbaeus suggest a childlike tenderness. What does Jesus say in this passage about having a heart "as a little child"?

_____

_____

_____

_____

_____

- Read John 14:19–24. What did Jesus say that caused Judas to ask why He would make Himself known to the disciples but not to the whole world? How do you think Jesus' answer reassured Judas that He was not overlooking those who honestly sought to follow Him?

  _____

  _____

  _____

  _____

- Read Luke 15:8–10. Jesus did not come as the Messiah to take over the world externally (as many of the Jews expected) but to take over one heart at a time. What does this parable say about God's joy when even a *single* sinner repents?

  _____

  _____

  _____

  _____

- Judas Lebbaeus Thaddaeus was motivated to quietly serve the Lord and preach the gospel. What are your motivations when it comes to quietly serving the Lord and sharing about Christ?

  _____

  _____

  _____

  _____

CONSIDERING YOUR STORY

Read Matthew 8:18–22. The disciples were an intriguing group of men who had a variety of personalities in the mix. Yet they all shared at least one thing in common.

● Many people who witnessed Jesus' miracles wanted to follow Him—but either the cost was too high or they had competing priorities. What do we know for certain about what the twelve disciples shared in common when it came to their commitment to Jesus?

_____

_____

_____

_____

_____

● What keeps you committed to following after Jesus? How do your fellow brothers and sisters in Christ—in whatever walks of life they come from—help you in this?

_____

_____

_____

_____

_____

● Take a moment to apply what you have learned about the lesser-known trio of James the Less, Simon the Zealot, and Judas (not Iscariot).

James the Less: What is one way that you are "quietly" serving God?

Simon the Zealot: How are you seeking after God above all else?

Judas (not Iscariot): How are you seeking to make your own name in God's kingdom?

APPLYING YOUR STORY

Jesus told His disciples, "Let your light so shine before men, that they may see your good works and glorify your Father in heaven" (Matthew 5:16). The goal is to make God's name famous on earth—not our own. What is one way today you can let your "light shine" to others?

_____

_____

_____

_____

_____

_____

_____

CLOSING PRAYER

Heavenly Father, You loved me before the world began, and Your love will sustain me to the end. Thank You for knowing my mind and for seeing my heart even when I don't understand Your purposes. Draw me back to You and Your love if I start to lose my way. My heart's desire is to proclaim Your name rather than my own. Please use me for Your glory. Amen.

Notes
1. John MacArthur, *Twelve Ordinary Men* (Nashville, TN: Thomas Nelson, 2002), 174.
2. MacArthur, *Twelve Ordinary Men*, 177.
3. Josephus (AD 37–100), *Antiquities of the Jews*, xviii.
4. Josephus, *Wars of the Jews*, iv.
5. MacArthur, *Twelve Ordinary Men*, 178–179.

JUDAS

THE TRAITOR

Jesus answered them, "Did I not choose you, the twelve,
and one of you is a devil?" He spoke of Judas Iscariot, the son of Simon,
for it was he who would betray Him.

JOHN 6:70-71

His name is as infamous as it is notorious. He has been depicted in countless works of art across the centuries, often sulking in the shadows as he plots how to hand over his Lord for a handful of coins. Judas Iscariot. In every mention of his name in the Bible, he is designated a traitor and a betrayer. But not just a betrayer—he is *the* betrayer. Judas spent three years with Jesus, like the rest of the disciples, but in all that time his heart only grew more hateful. His dark story poignantly illustrates the depths to which the human heart can sink.

Judas began like the other disciples. He was just a common man eager to follow the Messiah, whom he clearly assumed would be a political force for the restoration of Israel. Tragically, though, Judas had no interest in Jesus' priorities and no interest in loving or serving Him. His heart and mind were on other things. Time and again, in spite of many opportunities to turn from his ways, he chose the kingdom of darkness over the kingdom of light.

His life stands as a warning about the stark realities of spiritual coldness, worldly lusts, and hardness of heart. Here was a man who lived in the presence of the Savior and enjoyed the privilege of having direct access to Christ. He was a witness to everything Jesus taught and all the good works that He did. He even knew that Jesus was God—exactly as He had claimed.

Yet Judas never laid hold of the truth by faith, and so he was never transformed. While the other disciples were increasing in faith as sons of God, he was becoming more and more a child of hell. In the end, he remained in unbelief and entered a hopeless eternity. His life is a lesson in tragedy and lost opportunities. He is the epitome of wasted privilege. He is a classic illustration of how the love of money leads to destruction (see 1 Timothy 6:9). He is a vivid example of the deceitfulness and fruitfulness of hypocrisy.

Still, what we find in Judas's story is that God's love always triumphs. At first glance, his betrayal of Jesus appears to be among Satan's greatest triumphs. But what we find instead is that even the worst act of treachery will work toward the divine fulfillment of God's plan. The story of Judas trumpets an indisputable truth: No matter how cunning one's scheme, how cruel one's intent, or how deep one's hatred, God's plan of salvation cannot be thwarted.

STARTING OUT

What initially drew you to follow after Jesus? How has your initial interest in Him progressed or deepened as you have grown closer to Him day by day?

_____

_____

_____

_____

_____

_____

_____

EXPLORING THE STORY

Judas gave up his *life* to follow Jesus full-time. Sadly, he never gave Jesus his *heart*. He was a man who possessed *consuming avarice*, which led to his *cold betrayal* of Jesus, which in turn led to his *bitter end*. You will explore each of these aspects of his life in this section.

Consuming Avarice

Judas's name appears last in every biblical list of apostles (except in Acts 1:13, where it does not appear at all). His surname, Iscariot, is derived from the Hebrew *ish* (meaning "man") and a town named Kerioth. Thus, he was a "man of Kerioth," likely Kerioth-Hezron (see Joshua 15:25), a town in southern Judea. He appears to have been the lone disciple who did not come from Galilee—the outsider of the bunch. Meanwhile, as we know, many of the disciples knew each other as brothers, friends, or working companions prior to meeting Jesus.

The disciples were drawn to Jesus as a person. However, Judas saw Jesus as nothing more than a means to an end. At the start, he was no doubt attracted to what he expected to be the advent of an earthly, political, military, and economic kingdom. Jesus was the obvious fulfillment of the Old Testament messianic promises. He spoke, taught, and lived like no one else. Furthermore, Jesus had powers like no other man. What young, zealous, patriotic Jew *wouldn't* want to join such a leader in overthrowing Israel's Roman oppressors?

Judas and the other disciples shared the expectation that they would be rewarded for following Jesus (see Matthew 19:27). They anticipated material rewards in the here and now, unaware that their greatest reward would be in the age to come (see Luke 18:29–30). Over time, they began to realize that Jesus was not the Messiah they expected. However, rather than feeling disillusioned—as Judas apparently did—the eleven grew to love Jesus even more. Gradually, their love for Christ overcame their worldly ambitions. They grew to embrace His eternal values and teachings. His mission became their own.

By contrast, Judas grew disgruntled with Jesus' mission. For the most part, he hid his disappointment under a blanket of hypocrisy, continuing to act like a devoted disciple while pilfering money (see John 12:6) and seeking opportunities to capitalize on Jesus' prestige. However, his avarice and greed were exposed during a dinner at the home of Simon the Leper in Bethany (see Matthew 26:6). While

"A POUND OF VERY COSTLY OIL"

The term used for *pound* actually indicates a weight around three-fourths of a pound (approximately twelve ounces). *Spikenard* was an oil extracted from the root of a plant grown in India. Since those who were eating reclined at the table, their feet extended away from it, making it possible for Mary to anoint the feet of Jesus with the oil. The act symbolized Mary's humble devotion and love for Him.[1]

Jesus was at the table, Mary (the sibling of Martha and Lazarus) "took a pound of very costly oil of spikenard, anointed the feet of Jesus, and wiped His feet with her hair. And the house was filled with the fragrance of the oil" (John 12:3).

The extravagant act shocked the disciples. Jesus understood it as a joyous expression of worship. Judas saw it as gross excess. He said, "Why was this fragrant oil not sold for three hundred denarii [approximately a year's wages] and given to the poor?" (verse 5). Evidently, his criticism seemed reasonable to the other disciples, for they echoed his indignation (see Matthew 26:8). In truth, Judas was a thief who wanted that money for himself.

Jesus only lightly reprimanded Judas: "Let her alone; she has kept this for the day of My burial" (John 12:7). However, the incident seems to have been a turning point for Judas. He already resented Jesus for not being a political Savior. Now, Jesus' willingness to receive such lavish worship was costing him money that he could have skimmed from their treasury. Judas went to the chief priests and asked, "What are you willing to give me if I deliver Him to you?" (Matthew 26:15). They offered him thirty pieces of silver—the price of a slave (see Exodus 21:32). The contrast is staggering. At the same time that Mary anointed the Lord with overwhelming love, Judas was plotting to betray Him with overwhelming hate.

● Read John 12:1–8. What was Judas's role among the disciples? How did he reveal his avarice—his extreme greed for material wealth—in this story?

_____

_____

_____

_____

- Read John 15:1–6. Judas chose to live in deceit rather than abide in Christ. What does Jesus say will happen to a person who makes that same choice?

  _____

  _____

  _____

  _____

- Read Matthew 6:19–21 and Luke 12:15–21. What warnings did Jesus give about the love of money? What does it mean to lay up treasures in heaven rather than on earth?

  _____

  _____

  _____

  _____

- What are some ways that you are laying up treasures in heaven rather than on earth?

  _____

  _____

  _____

  _____

Cold Betrayal

Judas, having taken money for the betrayal, joined the other disciples to share in the Passover feast. Before they ate, Jesus washed each man's feet—even Judas's feet. The betrayer let Him do it, unmoved by Jesus' example of humility.

During the meal, Jesus said, "You are clean, but not all of you" (John 13:10b). He then specified, "I do not speak concerning all of you" (verse 18). He then spoke even more plainly: "Most assuredly, I say to you, one of you will betray Me" (verse 21). Matthew writes that all the disciples (except Judas) "were exceedingly sorrowful" and "each of them began to say to Him, 'Lord, is it I?'" (26:22). Judas, careful to keep up the ruse, chimed in, "Rabbi, is it I?" (verse 25).

However, in his case there had been no sincere self-examination. He asked the question only to keep the focus off himself. John reports that Jesus dipped a piece of bread in the wine and gave it to Judas, signifying he was the betrayer. At this point, "Satan entered him. Then Jesus said to him, 'What you do, do quickly.' . . . Having received the piece of bread, he then went out immediately. And it was night" (John 13:27, 30).

In that moment, the day of salvation closed for Judas. The darkness of sin triumphed in his heart—and Satan moved in. Judas's conspiracy soon came to fruition in the garden of Gethsemane. Jesus had just spent hours pouring out His heart to His Father. Suddenly, Judas arrived with a contingent of people, including "a detachment of troops," and they were carrying "lanterns, torches, and weapons" (John 18:3). This detachment of troops was most likely a Roman cohort—about six hundred men in total.

Jesus did not give Judas the chance to single Him out. "Jesus therefore, knowing all things that would come upon Him, went forward and said to them, 'Whom are you seeking?'" (verse 4). When the cohort answered, "Jesus of Nazareth," He then said, "I am He" (verse 5). Judas had arranged a signal to identify Jesus: "Whomever I kiss, He is the One; seize Him" (Matthew 26:48). However, because

BETRAYED WITH A KISS

In addition to being a special act of respect and affection, the kind of kiss that Judas gave to Jesus was a sign of homage in Middle Eastern culture. Out of the varieties of this kiss (on the feet, on the back of the hand, on the palm, on the hem of the garment), Judas chose the embrace and the kiss on the cheek—the one that showed the closest love and affection, normally reserved for one with whom a person had a close, intimate relationship (such as a pupil for his teacher). Judas could not have chosen a more despicable way to identify Jesus, because he perverted its usual meaning so treacherously and hypocritically.[2]

Jesus had been so quick in identifying Himself, the signal was unnecessary. Judas, the cynic and scoundrel, kissed Him anyway (see Mark 14:45). It was the worst kind of treachery, for with it, he profaned Jesus and betrayed his Lord.

● Read John 13:21–30. How did Peter and John react to Jesus' announcement that one of the disciples would betray Him? Why did none of them understand this betrayer was Judas?

_____

_____

_____

_____

_____

_____

● Read 1 Corinthians 11:27–29. Each of the disciples at the Last Supper, with the exception of Judas, engaged in *honest* self-examination. According to Paul, why is this necessary?

_____

_____

_____

_____

_____

_____

● Read 1 Peter 3:10–12. What does Peter say in this passage about not speaking with deceit? What is the promise for those who seek after righteousness?

_____

_____

_____

_____

_____

- David prayed, "Search me, O God, and know my heart" (Psalm 139:23). What are some ways that you engage in regular self-examination and ask God to search your heart?

_____

_____

_____

_____

_____

_____

Bitter End

Judas had handed Jesus over to the authorities. But with the deed done, his conscience suddenly came alive. "Judas . . . was remorseful and brought back the thirty pieces of silver to the chief priests and elders, saying, 'I have sinned by betraying innocent blood'" (Matthew 27:3–4a). His remorse was not the same as repentance. He was sorry not because he had sinned but because his sin did not satisfy him as he had hoped.

When Judas tried to return the money to the chief priests and elders, their response was unsympathetic. They had what they wanted—leaving Judas in a hell of his own making. Sadly, Judas did not seek God's forgiveness or cry for mercy. Instead, "he threw down the pieces of silver in the temple and departed, and went and hanged himself" (verse 5).

Apparently, Judas chose a tree on an overhang above some jagged rocks in a field. Either the rope snapped or the tree branch broke, and Judas fell headlong onto the rocks (see Acts 1:18–19). The Bible's last word about him is that "he burst open in the middle and all his entrails gushed out" (verse 18). Both Judas's life and his death were sickening tragedies. He was a child of hell and a son of perdition, and he went "to his own place" (verse 25).

Judas's betrayal of Jesus brought about the events that led to His death on the cross. It seemed as if hell had finally won. (Jesus' disciples certainly thought so in the days immediately after Jesus' death.) But, in truth, Judas's betrayal signaled the utter defeat for the evil one and all his plans (see Hebrews 2:14–18; 1 John 3:8). The victory was so great that not even the loss of one of the twelve disciples could prevent the gospel from going forward.

A Tragedy of His own Making

When Judas bartered away the life of Christ, he was in effect selling his own soul to the devil. The tragedy of his life was a tragedy of his own making. He ignored the light he had been exposed to for all those years he had spent with Jesus, and thus he relegated himself to eternal darkness. Hypocrites like Judas have no one but themselves to blame for the destruction of their souls.[3]

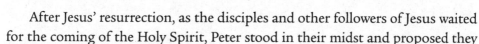

After Jesus' resurrection, as the disciples and other followers of Jesus waited for the coming of the Holy Spirit, Peter stood in their midst and proposed they find another to fill Judas's office (see Acts 1:15-22). Two names were put forth, and a man named Matthias was chosen (see verses 23-26). He was a dedicated believer who had been with Jesus and the other apostles "from the baptism of John to that day when He was taken up" (verse 22).

Nothing else is known of Matthias. Various traditions say he ministered in Ethiopia, or traveled to Damascus, or remained in Jerusalem. But the Bible is silent about the rest of his actions. What we *can* say is that he also became a powerful witness of Jesus' resurrection—one more ordinary man whom the Lord elevated to an extraordinary calling.

● Read 2 Corinthians 7:8-10. Judas expressed remorse for his actions—but not repentance. How does Paul explain the difference between the two?

_____

_____

_____

_____

_____

_____

_____

_____

_____

● Read 1 John 1:8–9. Judas was remorseful that his betrayal of Jesus did not satisfy him in the way he had hoped but did not seek God's forgiveness for his sins. What does John say that God is "faithful and just" to do when we genuinely repent of our sins?

_____

_____

_____

_____

_____

_____

● Read Colossians 2:13–14. Judas's betrayal of Jesus appeared to be a great victory for Satan. However, what does Paul say Jesus' death accomplished at the cross?

_____

_____

_____

_____

_____

● What stands out to you about the life of Judas Iscariot? What cautions from his story apply to every person who seeks to be a true follower of Jesus?

_____

_____

_____

_____

_____

_____

CONSIDERING YOUR STORY

Read Hebrews 3:7-14. It is a tragedy that Judas spent some three years in the very presence of Jesus and yet, in all that time, his heart was only growing harder and more hateful.

- Judas's life is a sober reminder that it is possible to closely associate with Jesus and His people and still become hardened by sin. Has there been a time in your life when you rebelled against God or rejected Him? Did you do so openly or hide behind hypocrisy?

  _____
  _____
  _____
  _____
  _____
  _____

- What turned your heart back toward God? How did He use other believers to help you?

  _____
  _____
  _____
  _____
  _____
  _____

- The author of Hebrews instructs us to "exhort one another daily" (verse 13). What are three practical ways that you believe God is using you to encourage others in their faith?

  1. _____
  2. _____
  3. _____

APPLYING TO YOUR LIFE

Jesus longs for His followers to come to Him with their disappointments or disillusionments. It takes little for the evil one to gain a foothold. Where does your heart need help today to stay tender toward God? Where do you need strengthening, comfort, or forgiveness?

_____

_____

_____

_____

_____

_____

_____

_____

_____

_____

_____

_____

CLOSING PRAYER

Jesus, You know the secret places in my heart where I hang on to grudges, sinful desires, and hurts. I do not want to be a person like Judas who rejects You and grows cold. Thank You for Your patience and Your love. Please turn me around, redirect my desires, and give me a fire for You. Do for me what I cannot do for myself. I ask for this in Your redeeming name. Amen.

Notes

1. John MacArthur, author and general editor, *The MacArthur Study Bible* (Nashville, TN: Thomas Nelson, 1997), note on John 12:3.

2. MacArthur, *The MacArthur Study Bible*, note on Mark 14:44.

3. MacArthur, *Twelve Ordinary Men*, 198.

ABOUT JOHN MACARTHUR

John MacArthur is the pastor-teacher of Grace Community Church in Sun Valley, California, as well as an author, conference speaker, chancellor of The Master's University and Seminary, and featured teacher with the Grace to You media ministry. After graduating from Talbot Theological Seminary, John came to Grace Community Church in 1969. Today, several thousand members participate every week at Grace Community Church in dozens of fellowship groups and training programs, most led by lay leaders and each dedicated to equipping members for ministry on local, national, and international levels.

In 1985, John became president of The Master's College (formerly Los Angeles Baptist College; since 2016, The Master's University). Located in Santa Clarita, California, it is a distinctly Christian, accredited, liberal arts institution offering undergraduate and graduate degree programs. In 1986, John founded The Master's Seminary, a graduate school dedicated to training men for full-time pastoral and missionary work.

John is also chairman and featured teacher with Grace to You. Founded in 1969, Grace to You is the nonprofit organization responsible for developing, producing, and distributing John's books, audio resources, and the Grace to You radio and television programs. Grace to You radio airs more than 1,000 times daily throughout the English-speaking world, reaching population centers with biblical truth. It also airs over 1,000 times a day in Spanish, reaching twenty-seven countries across Europe and Latin America.

John has written hundreds of study guides and books, including *The Gospel According to Jesus*, *Our Sufficiency in Christ*, *Strange Fire*, *Ashamed of the Gospel*, *The Murder of Jesus*, *The Prodigal Son*, *Twelve Ordinary Men*, *Twelve Extraordinary Women*, *The Truth War*, *The Jesus You Can't Ignore*, *Slave*, *One Perfect Life*, *The Gospel According to Paul*, *Parables*, and *One Faithful Life*. John's books have been translated into more than two dozen languages. The MacArthur Study Bible, the cornerstone resource of his ministry, is available in English (NKJV, NASB, and ESV), Spanish, Russian, German, French, Portuguese, Italian, Arabic, and Chinese.

John and his wife, Patricia, live in Southern California and have four married children: Matt, Marcy, Mark, and Melinda. They also enjoy the enthusiastic company of their fifteen grandchildren.

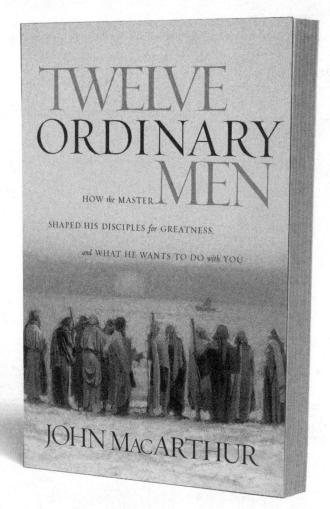

GENESIS 1-11
CREATION, SIN, AND THE NATURE OF GOD

ALSO AVAILABLE FROM

JOHN MACARTHUR

THE MACARTHUR BIBLE STUDY SERIES

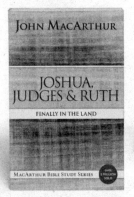

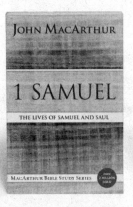

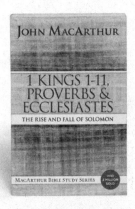

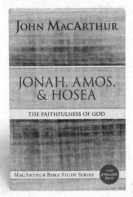

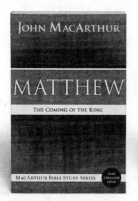

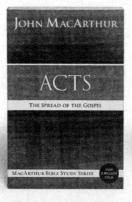

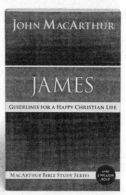

BIBLE STUDIES INCLUDE:

Genesis 1–11
Genesis 12–33
Genesis 34–50
Exodus & Numbers
Leviticus & Deuteronomy
Joshua, Judges & Ruth
1 Samuel
2 Samuel
1 Kings 1–11, Proverbs &
    Ecclesiastes
1 Kings 12–22
2 Kings
Ezra & Nehemiah
Daniel & Esther
Job
Psalms
Isaiah
Jeremiah & Lamentations
Ezekiel
Jonah, Amos & Hosea
Micah, Zephaniah, Nahum,
    Habakkuk, Joel & Obadiah
Zechariah, Haggai & Malachi

Matthew
Mark
Luke
John
Acts
Romans
1 Corinthians
2 Corinthians
Galatians
Ephesians
Philippians
Colossians & Philemon
1 & 2 Thessalonians & Titus
1 & Timothy
Hebrews
James
1 & 2 Peter
1, 2, 3 John & Jude
Revelation

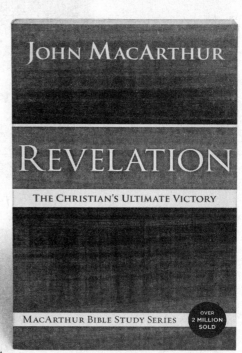

SCAN ME

HARPERCHRISTIANRESOURCES.COM

ALSO FROM
JOHN MACARTHUR

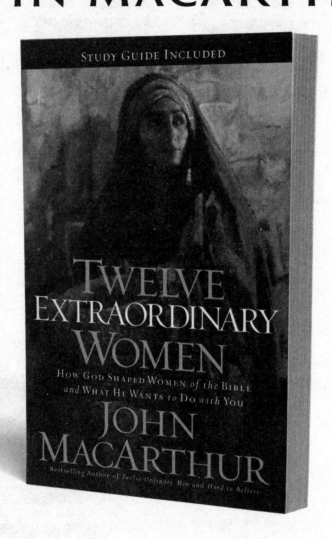

AVAILABLE WHEREVER BOOKS ARE SOLD.

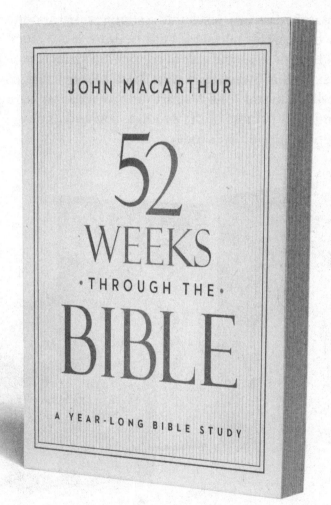

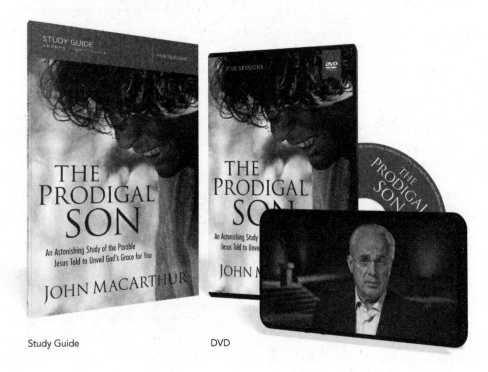

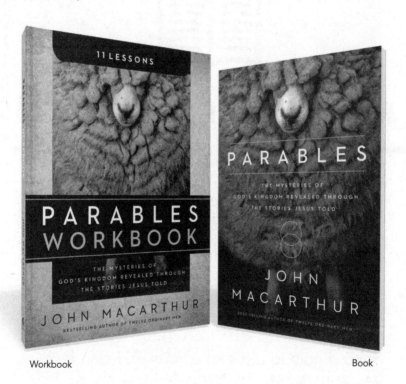